Competition and Antitrust Law: A Very Short Introduction

VERY SHORT INTRODUCTIONS are for anyone wanting a stimulating
and accessible way into a new subject. They are written by experts, and
have been translated into more than 45 different languages.

The series began in 1995, and now covers a wide variety of topics in
every discipline. The VSI library currently contains over 650 volumes—a
Very Short Introduction to everything from Psychology and Philosophy of
Science to American History and Relativity—and continues to grow in every
subject area.

Very Short Introductions available now:

Available soon:

For more information visit our website

www.oup.com/vsi/

Ariel Ezrachi

COMPETITION AND ANTITRUST LAW

A Very Short Introduction

Great Clarendon Street, Oxford, OX2 6DP,
United Kingdom

Oxford University Press is a department of the University of Oxford.
It furthers the University's objective of excellence in research, scholarship,
and education by publishing worldwide. Oxford is a registered trade mark of
Oxford University Press in the UK and in certain other countries

Published in the United States of America by Oxford University Press
198 Madison Avenue, New York, NY 10016, United States of America

British Library Cataloguing in Publication Data
Data available

Library of Congress Control Number: 2021931423

ISBN 978–0–19–886030–3

Printed and bound by
CPI Group (UK) Ltd, Croydon, CR0 4YY

Contents

List of illustrations

Introduction

Look around you. You are most likely sitting comfortably on a chair or sofa, in a heated or cooled room, surrounded by your comfort technology—from your smart water-resistant mobile phone, to your new extra thin laptop with its long-life battery. As you read this Introduction, you might be interrupted by notices on your phone, video chats from friends, and reminders from your digital assistant. You might then step out and go to your favourite shop, where choice is abundant, to buy reasonably priced food and goods. You might later meet friends in your favourite hangout where the service is excellent. Maybe you will travel around town in your reasonably priced car or ride sharing service, watch a movie, or just explore the market.

Your environment is characterized by ample choice, smiling service providers, and reasonably priced goods. Sure, things can always improve. No doubt. But pause for a second and appreciate one of the key drivers that make this environment possible—the competitive process.

It is the rivalry between businesses and traders that delivers the abundance of choice, the lower prices, the increased innovation, and the better quality of goods and services. It is this process of competition which enables your money to go the extra step: to buy more for less. A process which has generated much of the prosperity of the Western world. Without it, you would most likely have been sitting in a somewhat bare room on an uncomfortable chair that was purchased from an unpleasant seller at an inflated price. Your money would buy you less. Fewer goods, fewer services, less quality, and less innovation. Not so rosy.

And so, as a society, we strive to protect the beneficial dynamics of competition as a means to enhance consumer welfare, deliver efficiencies, and encourage innovation.

At times, society has to work hard to maintain the abundance that comes with competition. While competition benefits us, the consumers, it makes the life of producers, sellers, and service providers rather difficult. They need to improve to stay in business. They need to invest in new products, new technologies, new processes. They need to offer us goods and services at an attractive price. If they fail to remain competitive, they may find themselves being pushed out of the market. And so, at times, these sellers and service providers may look for ways to dampen the competitive process. Think, for example, of price-fixing cartels or market sharing agreements which result in us paying more and getting less. Think of powerful companies that might abuse their power to distort the market, for example, by stopping their customer from buying from other companies. Or maybe large merger transactions between two giant companies that could leave us dealing with a single dominant seller that benefits from concentrated power.

Our antitrust and competition laws are designed to address these risks, remedy possible market failures, and safeguard consumer welfare. Our competition agencies and courts are tasked with enforcing the law. As they do so, they face the challenge of correctly identifying what amounts to an anti-competitive activity and curtailing it to ensure dynamic and competitive markets.

This book is about these market dynamics, their promises and limitations. It is about the laws that are used to safeguard the process of competition, and the way they are enforced. About the delicate and challenging relationship between a free market economy and government intervention. It is about the fascinating forces of competition that influence your wealth and shape our modern society.

Chapter 1
The power of competition

For centuries economists and policy makers have examined how companies compete for business and how competition benefits society. You've probably heard of the Scottish economist Adam Smith whose metaphor of the 'invisible hand (of competition)' is still used today to illustrate the dynamics of markets. It explains how sellers in a competitive market will try to earn more money by reducing the price of products and services to attract more customers. Similarly, they will invest in better services and quality. Sellers know that if they provide poor service or poor quality, or charge high prices, we will take our business elsewhere. So, they compete fiercely. The unintended social benefit of their actions is a more efficient market where consumer welfare increases—that is, we get more and pay less.

As you walk along the high street or shop online, you may notice how markets for different goods and services differ from each other. Some are highly competitive—they offer a choice of high-quality products at lower prices. In others, there is limited choice and prices seem rather excessive. The nature of the product and the structure of the market affect the intensity of competition and subsequently the price and quality of goods and services.

To see how market structure affects competition, let's begin by looking at the model of perfect competition:

Perfect competition

The model of perfect competition illustrates the ideal market scenario—a perfect market which maximizes consumer welfare. Imagine a vast marketplace with endless sellers, all competing for your business. Competition in this market is fierce. New competitors easily join the market every day, as there are no barriers to entry. As they join, they try to outperform the existing sellers. Those who are unable to compete effectively are driven out of the market. In this market, only those who provide the best-quality product at the lowest price (with the best service) can survive. To make money, sellers continuously invest in improving production and distribution. If they become more efficient, they can lower the price. When they do, more customers buy from them. Failure to improve the quality of goods and services, to increase efficiencies and offer the lowest price, results in sellers being pushed out of the market. In such a reality, sellers cannot afford to rest. They must innovate and improve daily. They must attract our business.

In a perfectly competitive market, the customer is completely informed and knows exactly which seller has the best quality and lowest price. Consumers are rational and can easily identify the best bargain to suit their needs. The market is simple, with homogeneous products that make it easy for customers to get the best bargain.

Sellers are also well informed and can maximize their output. They can easily enter the market to compete against the incumbents; they can easily expand their business when they succeed; and, if they fail to succeed, they can leave the market, without incurring sunk costs, to try their luck in another market.

And so, in a perfectly competitive market, consumers are king. The market maximizes their welfare and the overall welfare of society. The invisible hand of competition operates in full force, delivering efficiencies and welfare. Market dynamics determine the price and no seller benefits from power which could be used to distort competition or exploit consumers.

The model of perfect competition provides us with a valuable image. But as you may have suspected, while conceptually valuable, the model differs from reality. Life and markets, as we experience them, are more complicated and many of the assumptions at the core of the model are not always present. Think, for example, about information flows that are often imperfect (think of all the times you thought you had got the best bargain, only to discover that a better one existed just around the corner); think about complex markets with heterogeneous products, brands, and loyalty programmes that make it harder for us to make a choice; or about the many barriers that make it difficult and costly for sellers to enter some markets (regulation, taxation, investment). Real markets, even when they work well, are somewhat imperfect. However, despite its limitations and oversimplification, the model offers us an illustration of the ideal to strive for. It also helps us appreciate competitive markets when we see them.

Monopoly

Having considered the ideal at one end of the 'competition spectrum', let us now look at the other extreme end, and consider the consequences of limited competition in a market dominated by a monopoly. In such a market, a single firm offers the product or service. No other competitors operate in the market, and consumers who desire the product have to purchase it from the monopolist. The market has high barriers to entry, which act like fences to prevent others from entering. These fences may be the result of state laws, technology, or high investment required to enter the market. Either way, they shield the monopolists from challengers. Our monopolist faces no potential competition, no threat of entry of other providers, and subsequently no competitive pressure.

In such an extreme market reality, the monopolist can restrict output and thereby increase the price of goods and services. Living the easy, and somewhat lazy, life, the monopolist will invest less in efficiencies and innovation, ultimately dedicating less attention to offering customers a better service. Customers are faced with no outside options—no alternative sellers that can satisfy their needs. They are 'locked in' with the monopolist and have to pay more for lower quality goods and services.

We can see how our welfare is undermined in such a market. Of course, this extreme end of the spectrum is not often reflective of reality. Many times, even the most powerful companies will face some competitive pressure, some risk of entry by others, or some uncertainty, that will encourage them to restrain their actions. Still, understanding the extreme point of the spectrum helps us to appreciate the consequences of market power and its welfare implications.

One caveat is in order at this point. While in the overwhelming majority of cases, monopolistic markets deliver lower value and reduce consumer welfare, this might not be the case in circumstances involving a *natural monopoly*. In some unique markets, society may benefit from having a single powerful company fulfil the entire market's demand for its product or service. This could be the case where developing a service offering involves such large fixed costs and economies of scale, that duplicating this cost over two or more service providers actually outweighs the benefits to customers from increased competition. Natural monopoly markets may include utilities such as water or electricity delivery, railroads, and other infrastructure. In these markets it is possible that a single provider might be able to offer greater efficiencies and welfare than could be achieved through competitive dynamics. Of course, natural monopolies must still share their efficiency benefits with society. In the absence of competitive pressure, such markets will often be regulated to ensure that consumer interest is protected, for example, by determining the price customers are being charged. Sometimes, the state will introduce structured competition into these market through, for example, requiring investors to 'bid' on natural monopoly rights and thereby compete on the opportunity to be the service provider.

Oligopoly

The two key models described above—*perfect competition* and *monopoly*—illustrate the two ends of the competitiveness spectrum. Along this spectrum we may find a range of market structures that differ in their key characteristics. They may exhibit varying levels of concentration (that is, a different number of companies operating in the market), varying degrees of product homogeneity (how differentiated are products in the market), different levels of market transparency, different entry barriers, and different seller and buyer power. Markets on that spectrum will yield *imperfect competition* that will vary based on the market's unique characteristics.

To illustrate an imperfect competitive dynamic, let's look at a type of market called an oligopoly.

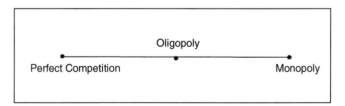

An oligopoly is a market characterized by a few key competitors. Sometimes, the market may exhibit rivalry between the firms as they engage in price wars and try to steal each other's customers or invest heavily in innovation. At other times, however, oligopolistic markets may exhibit limited competition. This may be the case when an oligopolistic market with few competitors is transparent and stable, and there is limited threat of new entry. In such instances a phenomenon known as 'tacit collusion' or 'conscious parallelism' may emerge, resulting in limited competitive pressure and interdependence among market players. In its judgment in *Brooke Group Ltd v Brown & Williamson Tobacco Corp.*, the United States Supreme Court explained this phenomenon:

> [T]acit collusion, sometimes called oligopolistic price coordination or conscious parallelism, describes the process, not in itself unlawful, by which firms in a concentrated market might in effect share monopoly power, setting their prices at a profit-maximizing, supracompetitive level by recognizing their shared economic interests and their interdependence with respect to price and output decisions and subsequently unilaterally set their prices above the competitive level.

Importantly, tacit collusion may result in higher prices without involving any illegal communications or collusion between the companies. The parallel behaviour alone, which may stem from tacit collusion, is legal.

To illustrate this phenomenon, let us consider the gas (petrol) market in Martha's Vineyard island, located in the United States. Residents on the island were angered by the prices they were charged at gas stations, which were distinctively higher than those in the nearby Cape Cod peninsula. These high prices, the residents argued in the case of *William WHITE et al. v R.M. PACKER CO., INC.*, were the result of illegal price coordination.

The trial and appellate courts considered these allegations and the possibility that the high prices were the natural result of the market characteristics rather than illegal price coordination.

Following an examination of the petrol market in Martha's Vineyard, the court concluded that it had the characteristics which would facilitate conscious parallelism. The market had a small number of companies operating gas stations and was characterized by high regulatory barriers that prevented new stations from entering and operating on the island. Customers (drivers) had limited outside options. When travelling on the island they had to buy gas/petrol and could not simply stay out of the market until prices dropped (or alternatively drive to another island). Petrol prices were transparent, a fact that enabled each station to adjust its pricing to changes implemented by its competitors.

These conditions gave rise to interdependence, as stations refrained from discounting and followed each other's price increases. As noted by the court:

> Since there are only nine gas stations on the entire island, each station can easily monitor and respond to the prices of the others. If one station drops its price in order to attract more business, the others can quickly drop their prices in response. The original 'cheater' benefits very little from undercutting its competitors' prices, because when any one of them drops its prices the competitors can match the price before many customers respond to the incentive. And all of the stations suffer a decrease in profit margin. Conversely, a station acting as a price 'leader' risks little by raising its price under such market conditions. Other stations are likely to follow, given the possibility of higher prices and profit margins for all. If for some reason the competitors do not follow the increases, the leader can easily drop its price again to match the other stations so quickly that few customers are lost to lower-priced competition. Knowing these features of the market, each gas station owner is likely to reach its own independent conclusion that its best interests involve keeping prices high, including following price changes by a price 'leader' (if one emerges), in confidence that the other station owners will reach the same independent conclusion.

Let's explain the mechanism at the heart of conscious parallelism. Imagine that each gas station in Martha's Vineyard sells 10 units of petrol per week at a price of $10 (making revenues of $100 per week). Remember that this market is characterized by transparency (competitors can see each other's actions), barriers to entry (no threat of new competitors entering the market), and no buyer power (customers cannot force price reduction or sponsor a new entry).

Now imagine that one of the gas stations, X, decides to drop its price per unit to $8 to gain more customers and increase overall profitability. As X drops the price, each of the other competitors notes this immediately (as well as the fact that its customers are gravitating towards X). To address this, each competitor reacts by dropping its price to $8. At the end of the week, they each sold 10 units of petrol, but at a price of $8 (making revenues of $80 per week). Still attempting to win the competition, X drops the price further, to $7, and yet the others again match the price drop to retain their customers. They now each earn only $70 per week.

X realizes that, while in a competitive petrol market a reduction in price will likely attract more customers and increase profitability, this strategy does not work in this specific oligopolistic market. The competitors' ability to detect the price drop in the transparent market, and to react swiftly, resulted in mutual loss for all. The market is characterized by interdependence which undermines X's competitive strategy. Throughout this experience the other competitors will also learn that the market is characterized by interdependence. Each time a gas station tries to undercut the others' prices, the competitors will match this price cut. In other words, no one will profit by discounting their prices.

This not only reduces the gas stations' incentive to discount; it increases their incentive to follow a price rise. And so, as X increases the price back to $10, the others follow. They do so knowing that if any of them tries to undercut, the others will subsequently match them, and they will all lose. When the following week X announces its intention to increase its petrol price to $12, the others follow. They recognize their shared economic interests, and all benefit from a healthier profit margin.

Importantly, the parallelism described above, that 'stickiness' of pricing behaviour, was a natural reaction to market characteristics. The gas stations charge high prices without entering into illegal agreement or communication. All they have done is to act unilaterally and rationally, reacting to the market dynamic.

The result? In an oligopolistic market which exhibits the conditions for conscious parallelism, we would expect prices to be higher. Firms may still compete on quality and service, but, overall, customers will get less for their money.

Chapter 2
Markets

In Chapter 1, we considered a competitive spectrum ranging from perfect competition to monopoly. As we described the varying market characteristics and key models, we frequently made references to *markets*.

But what exactly happens in a market once buyers and sellers interact? How is price determined? How do we know which products are included in a market and whether that market is dominated by one company or many?

In this chapter we will try to answer these questions by looking at demand and supply, and subsequently the way we define a relevant market.

Consumer demand for products

Your demand for a given product—your willingness to pay for it—is likely affected by the product characteristics, the availability of other products that act as substitutes, and the available money in your pocket (your income).

Like you, many others may be interested in that product, yet everyone differs slightly in their willingness to pay. Think for example of the most recent hi-tech gadget released to the market.

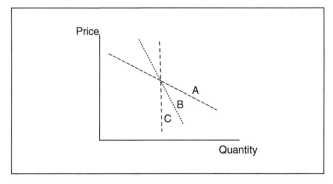

1. Demand curves

Some will be very eager and willing to pay a lot to use this gadget. Others may be relatively price sensitive and would only buy it at a lower price. At different price points, different people will be willing to buy the product.

Aggregating the data about these individuals generates a demand curve, which tells us how the demand for a given product changes with its price. As illustrated in Figure 1, that curve often slopes downwards, as more people are willing to buy the gadget as its price goes down.

The dotted line marked *A* illustrates the market demand for the gadget. Now let us add another product for which dotted line B illustrates the demand. The different slopes you notice represent differences in the *own-price elasticity of demand*—the different ways customers react to a change in price of a given product (this is known as PED—price elasticity of demand). For some products, we react to an increase in price by significantly limiting our demand. For others, we may be less price sensitive and exhibit only a limited fall in demand when faced with a price increase. Line B represents this less elastic demand for our new product. Now imagine a third product that you must buy regardless of its price. Such a product, like a lifesaving medicine, will have a completely inelastic demand, as it will be purchased regardless of the price. This is represented by the vertical line C.

Each of the three products in Figure 1 has a different price elasticity. In competition analysis we are often interested not only in a product's own-price elasticity, but also in *cross-price elasticity* which reflects the way in which a change in price for one product affects our demand for a similar product (this is known as XED—cross elasticity of demand). We will return to this term later, as we consider the definition of the market.

Before we move on, one additional fact is interesting to note. While the demand curves downwards in the illustration—indicating increased demand as price drops—that is not always the case. In some unique instances, demand may actually increase with price, as people desire the product more when its price increases. In such cases the demand curve will slope upwards. Such may be the case when considering luxury goods. An expensive brand may lose much of its shine if everyone can buy it cheaply. The demand for the brand may, in such a case, increase as its price is pushed upwards (up to a point...).

The supply of products and services

On the other side of the market, suppliers also exhibit different levels of willingness to produce and sell a product, based on the price customers will pay for it. If customers will only pay a low price, suppliers will make very few, if any, units available on the market. But where consumers are willing to pay a high price for a product, suppliers will increase their output of the product.

As with demand, we can illustrate how production of a product changes with its price using a supply curve. The curve illustrates the correlation between the product price and quantity available for a given period. The supply curve generally slopes upwards as

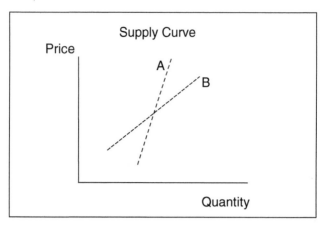

2. Supply curve

customers' willingness to pay increases, and the amount which suppliers produce follows. We can measure the responsiveness of the quantity supplied to a change in price and note different levels of *price elasticity of supply*. In Figure 2, line A represents a less elastic supply curve than line B.

The market price

Now take the demand curve and the supply curve and join them together. In a simplified scenario, the meeting point between the two, in a competitive market, represents the market price. That is the price at which producers are willing to sell a given quantity of a product and consumers are willing to buy it.

The market price represents an equilibrium that changes based on demand and supply characteristics. It is affected, among other things, by the nature of the product in question (lifesaving medicine, food, consumer products), by the availability and price of substitutions (cross-price elasticity), by changing consumer needs and preferences, by innovation, and by consumers' level of

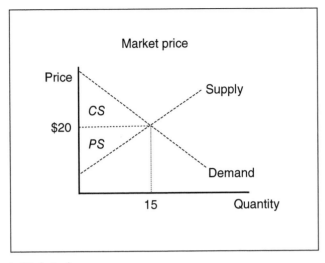

3. Market price

income. Figure 3 offers a simple illustration of the interface between supply and demand.

In our example, for a given product, an equilibrium was reached when suppliers offered fifteen units, which buyers purchased at a price of $20. Note that the market price is $20 and all customers who buy the product benefit from it. Even those customers who were willing to pay more for the product (those who are at the higher end of the demand curve) can benefit from the market price. The difference between the price that consumers are willing to pay and the price that they do pay results in *consumer surplus*. It is illustrated by the triangle between the market price and the demand curve (marked *CS*). Below that triangle is the area which symbolizes the *producer surplus*. That is, the difference between how much a producer would be willing to accept for a given quantity of a product and how much they actually receive when selling at the market price. It is illustrated by the triangle between the market price and the supply curve (marked *PS*).

Market definition

Having explained the core powers of demand and supply as well as their interaction, let us now explore what actually constitutes a market for a given product.

To define the market in question we embark on an inquiry in which we consider demand and supply characteristics to identify a group of products that form a relevant market. The key to the analysis lies in discovering which products customers are willing to substitute for each other in response to a change in price or quality.

If two products are deemed to act as viable substitutes for each other, then they exert competitive pressure on each other and as such belong to the same product market. If, on the other hand, a product is distinct and consumers will not view other products as viable substitutes, it may form the totality of the market. Sometimes products may be distinct due to their intrinsic characteristics, at other times it is the branding and heavy investment in advertising which may change our perception and result in us treating a given product as being entirely unique so that it cannot be substituted by others.

At times the market in question is evident—there is a clear product which is sold in a defined territory. At other times, the process may be complex and controversial, and it may not be clear which products and territories make up a market. As European Commissioner Margrethe Vestager noted:

> Defining markets isn't like agreeing the border between two countries, by drawing a line on a map. It's more like charting a coastline. The shape is already there—our job is just to measure it as accurately as we can. And nothing we do will change the shape of that coastline itself.

Market definition is not an end in itself. Once defined, the market scope helps us to identify boundaries of competition and consider market structure, market characteristics, the barriers to entry, the level of concentration, and the intensity of competition. The way we define the market may therefore affect our conclusion as to its competitiveness. It may affect the legal requirements that apply to companies operating on the market, and the likely enforcement actions that could follow.

The process of market definition is therefore of significance, as it helps us identify the boundaries of competition. Guidelines issued by competition agencies around the world have clearly defined the analytical process for defining markets. The United States (US) and European Union (EU) guidelines share analytical similarities and involve consideration of product and geographical markets.

The product market

The *product market* includes all those products which customers will substitute for each other in response to changes in price or quality. We will often consider the interchangeability of products by examining cross-price elasticity, which measures the percentage change in demand for one product or service after a change in the price of another.

The inquiry into the product market primarily focuses on demand substitutability. To analyse which products are substitutes, we can use a 'hypothetical monopolist' test. This test assumes that a monopoly produces all of a given type of product, and considers how customers would react to a 'small but significant non-transitory increase in price' for that product (this analysis is also known as the 'SSNIP test'). If enough customers respond to the price increase by purchasing an alternative product, then that product exerts competitive pressure on the original product, and the two products form part of the same product market. We then repeat this exercise until we find a set of products for which a price increase would be profitable for a hypothetical monopolist because consumers cannot simply switch to other products. At this point we would have identified the scope of the product market.

This may sound complicated, but it can be easily simplified by using an example. Think about boxed frozen margherita pizza bought in your local supermarket. Is there a market for frozen margherita pizza in which only companies that produce that pizza compete? Or is there a wider market for all types of frozen pizzas (margherita, pepperoni, four cheese, etc. . . .)? Or maybe frozen margherita pizza forms part of a wider product market, such as the market for all frozen readymade food, the market for frozen and chilled (not frozen) pizzas, or possibly the market for all pizzas (including delivery)?

To answer the question, we can apply the SSNIP test and ask how customers would react to a small increase in the price of frozen margherita pizza.

Think for a second. At the supermarket, when faced with an increase of 5–10 per cent in the price of frozen margherita pizza, might you consider purchasing another type of frozen pizza? Pepperoni, for example? If the answer is 'yes', the increase in price of frozen margherita pizza by a hypothetical monopolist would be unprofitable. Frozen pepperoni pizzas (or other types of frozen pizzas) serve as a viable substitute in the eyes of the customer and therefore form part of that market. If so, let's ask the same question again, now looking at a wider group of products. When faced with an increase in the price of various frozen pizzas, would you consider purchasing chilled pizza instead? If the answer is 'yes', chilled pizzas should be added to the market as they exert competitive pressure. As you continue asking the question, you aim to establish which products act as substitutes to our margherita pizza. The product market may include all frozen pizzas or maybe frozen and chilled pizzas, or maybe also delivery pizza or other fast foods. Again, and again, we ask the same question looking at additional substitutes. When we reach the answer 'no', we have identified the group of products that together form the relevant product market.

'Locked-in' and 'marginal' customers

In the example above we asked how *you* would react when faced with an increase in price of frozen margherita pizzas. That question was somewhat simplified, since in practice we do not determine the scope of the market based on one person's own preferences but on the preferences of a group of customers. If, for example, you like nothing more than frozen margherita pizza and will never consider any other pizza or food to act as a substitute, that in itself does not suggest that the market is narrow and only includes frozen margherita pizza. Our focus is not on the number of people who will never buy any other product, but rather on whether there are enough customers who would consider other products to act as substitutes.

Markets

Why? Because our aim is to identify if a group large enough might consider another product as a substitute to frozen margherita pizza so as to make a price increase by the hypothetical monopolists unprofitable.

We are not concerned with groups of customers who may be locked in due to preferences or loyalty. Our focus is on the marginal group that might consider buying alternative products. We therefore ask whether a sufficient number of customers would switch to another product to make a price increase unprofitable.

It is important not to confuse the marginal group with the locked-in group.

The European Court of Justice made this mistake in *United Brands*. In a case concerning United Brands' dominance in the market for bananas, the court ignored data suggesting that consumers switch between bananas and other fresh fruit based on price and availability of seasonal fresh fruit, and instead found a distinct market for bananas. The court reached this conclusion because a group of captive consumers consisting of the 'very young, the old, and the sick' had a constant need for a supply of bananas. These groups appreciated the bananas' softness, seedlessness, and easy handling. Focusing on the bananas' captive consumers led the court to observe and conclude that, when faced with an increase in price, this group would continue to buy bananas and so the market consists only of bananas. In reaching this conclusion, the court overlooked a large group of other customers who would happily switch from bananas to other fruit when faced with an increase in price (the marginal group). As long as that group is large enough, a small increase in the price of bananas by the hypothetical monopolists would be unprofitable. The price of bananas is constrained by other fruit that form part of the same market.

Again here, a caveat is in order, as sometimes the captive group could be relevant to the analysis when the hypothetical monopolists can isolate it and treat it differently from others. In *FTC v Whole Foods Market* the US Court of Appeal held that a submarket of core captive customers may exist when the monopoly can discriminate against those captive customers and extract monopoly profits from them while competing for the business of marginal customers.

The 'cellophane fallacy'

The SSNIP test provides a useful tool to assess the scope of the market by considering the reaction of customers to an increase in price. It is important to note that the test assumes that the prevailing price on the market is competitive before asking how customers would react to a small increase in price. If, however, we were to apply the test to a market price which is already inflated above a competitive level, it may fail to offer us credible conclusions as to the scope of the market. Why? Because when we ask how customers would react to a further increase in price on an already inflated price, we may conclude that they would use poor alternatives or products that would not act as substitutes under normal conditions. In such cases we may wrongly conclude that the product market is wider than it really is.

This phenomenon is commonly known as the *cellophane fallacy*, as it was first encountered in the US Supreme Court case of *US v E.I. Du Pont De Nemours & Co.* In that case, US antitrust enforcers alleged that Du Pont infringed antitrust law to sustain its monopoly over cellophane wrap, over which it had a 75 per cent market share. The US Supreme Court considered the relevant product market to be much wider, going beyond cellophane wrap. Applying the hypothetical monopolist test, the court held that Du Pont instead competed in a broader market for flexible packaging materials, which included things like aluminium foil and waxed paper, in which Du Pont had only a 20 per cent market share.

What led the court to conclude that this market is wide? The court applied the SSNIP test to the already inflated prices charged by Du Pont for cellophane wrap. The prices were so inflated that an additional price increase (as part of the SSNIP test) pushed consumers unwillingly onto other products which were poor substitutes.

The 'cellophane fallacy' highlights a significant shortcoming in the SSNIP test. When the market exhibits market power, the prevailing price may already be too high, and the test will result in false substitution. In such instances the test should be applied with caution (to the estimated competitive price), or give way to other methods which can be used to assess the boundaries of the market.

The geographical market

Having defined the product market, we need to identify the *geographical market*—the area in which the relevant product or service is sold and in which competition is 'sufficiently homogeneous'. Several factors may affect the scope of the geographical market: product characteristics such as perishability and volatility, distribution costs, regulation (for example, trade barriers or rules mandating certain product characteristics), third party intellectual property rights, licensing fees, customs, language, currency, price differences, transport costs as a proportion of overall value, and ability of consumers and suppliers to travel.

Let's illustrate with two cases:

In the matter of *DaVita, Inc.*, the US Federal Trade Commission (FTC) identified the product market as that of outpatient kidney dialysis treatment. It then moved on to consider the geographical market for outpatient kidney dialysis treatment. In its analysis the FTC took account of the distance patients can travel to receive treatment. It found that most patients were willing to travel no more than 30 miles or 30 minutes to receive dialysis treatment. It therefore identified geographical clusters separate from each other, each comprised of its own geographic market.

In the *United Brands* case, referenced earlier, the European Court of Justice considered the geographical market for bananas. Taking account of national regulations across Europe led the court to conclude that the geographic market for bananas consists of Germany, Denmark, Ireland, the Netherlands, and other localities which all had sufficiently similar conditions of competition in the market for bananas. By contrast, the United Kingdom (UK), France, and Italy all organized their banana markets nationally, using, for example, various quota systems which preferenced certain countries of origin.

Chains of substitutions

Often, the characteristics of the product will offer us a hint as to the scope of the geographical market. For example, a product which is easily transported and of high value is likely to have a wide market, possibly global. On the other hand, a product which is perishable, bulky, and relatively cheap, may be sold in regional markets, due to high transport costs. One would expect, for instance, the market for fresh milk or bread to be local in nature, but the market for diamonds or jet airplanes to be international.

However, even where product characteristics and high transport costs suggest a local market, *chains of substitution* can lead to an overall wider geographical scope. That may be the case where a product is supplied and consumed in overlapping localities, and consumers on the boundaries of these localities can choose from which place to source their product.

To illustrate how chains of substitution operate, let us assume that there is a distinct product market which includes delivery pizzas and let's consider its geographical scope. Delivery pizza is bulky, of relative low value, perishable, and requires rapid transportation. Its market is localized, usually a radius of up to 20 minutes' drive from the restaurant. In a world with few delivery outlets of pizza, we may identify geographical clusters separated from each other. Each will form a separate geographical market for delivery pizza. Each delivery outlet will have significant market power in its locality.

However, in a busy city with several outlets we may see how the radiuses created by various outlets can overlap. While some customers can only be served by one outlet, others can conveniently source their pizza from two or more restaurants. This overlap results in competitive pressure between the different outlets.

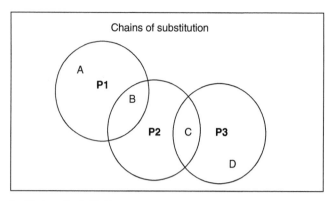

4. Chains of substitution

Figure 4 illustrates three pizza delivery outlets, each with a 20-minute drive radius around it. Customer group A can only be served by P1. Customer group B can benefit from deliveries from both P1 and P2. Customer group C can receive deliveries from P2 and P3. Customer group D can only be served by P3.

The overlap between the delivery areas turns what would otherwise be a narrow geographical market into a wider homogeneous regional market. Let's explain how: P1 delivers pizza to two groups of customers. However, while group A is locked in and can only order pizza from P1, group B has a choice of ordering from P1 or P2. An increase in the price by P1 of delivery pizza could push group B to order from P2. As long as group B is large enough, P1 will act swiftly to retain its business. P1 is therefore constrained by P2's pricing strategy. P2 is similarly constrained by P3 as it may lose customer group C if its price of pizza is too high.

The chain of substitution—that is, the overlap between the delivery territories—may enable group A to benefit from a discount pricing strategy implemented by P3 (although group A is not within its delivery range). When P3 introduces a discount to lure group C, P2 has to react with a similar discount to avoid losing business to P3. Group B benefits from that strategy and may shift all its demand to P2. To prevent it from ordering from P2, P1 will also drop its price. The result? Group A can enjoy a tasty pizza at a lower price, despite it being serviced by only a single delivery outlet. As long as P1 cannot discriminate against group A, the geographical market will include all three territories.

The significance of market definition

Having explored the definition of the product and geographical market, let's return to our frozen pizza example. In your opinion, what might be the product market? And the geographical market?

Your answer to these questions will determine your conclusion as to the market characteristics and the possible presence of market power. It affects your conclusion as to the number of companies operating in that market, the presence of barriers to expansion and entry, and the presence of potential competitors that operate outside the market but could potentially enter in the future. This, in turn, will affect your conclusions as to the concentration level in the market, the presence of market power, and the interrelationship between competitors. It could affect the conclusions as to the legality, and conformity with competition laws, of an agreement or a practice.

With so much at stake, it is little wonder that the debate about the boundaries of a given market in a given case is often the subject of controversy. It is prudent to treat the definition of the market as a valuable analytical framework but to refrain from attributing rigid boundaries to it prior to examining all the relevant factors.

Chapter 3
The goals and scope of competition and antitrust laws

In a world with perfect competition, markets would deliver an abundance of efficiencies and welfare. The invisible hand of competition would ensure that no seller would benefit from power which could enable it to distort competition or exploit consumers. In such a market, there would be little need for antitrust and competition laws.

In reality, many markets are less than perfect. Some businesses may try to limit the pressure of competition to increase their profitability. They could do this through illegal schemes (such as cartel agreements), through mergers, or by abusing their market power.

This is where competition and antitrust laws play an important role. States enact these laws to safeguard the process of competition and prevent companies from distorting it. Competition laws aim to ensure free and fair competition dynamics which can deliver consumer welfare and efficiencies.

Common goals

A look at the international landscape reveals consensus as to the main goals of competition laws. These laws seek to *protect the competitive process* in the marketplace from companies that seek to distort it.

By safeguarding free and dynamic markets, competition laws promote *consumer welfare*—that is, the benefits customers derive from consuming goods and services in a competitive environment. Competition law ensures that we get more out of our markets: that we get better products and services at lower prices.

Competition laws also aim to promote *efficiencies* in the marketplace. The law helps maintain a competitive environment, in which producers and sellers strive to win the competition and increase profitability. To do so, they seek to reduce costs and optimize efficiencies in production (production efficiency). They invest in research and innovation in the long run to improve their offerings, and win market share (dynamic efficiency). In a competitive market more efficient firms expand their operations, new efficient firms enter the market, and less efficient firms leave the market as they are unable to maintain profitability. Resources flow to the most efficient firms (allocative efficiency).

National variations

While key competition law principles are similar across the world, competition laws are not internationally uniform, but are instead customized by each jurisdiction. Each country may have different ideas as to the scope and role of competition law. This is because each jurisdiction designs its laws to promote certain values which reflect the ethos of each society at the time of enactment. Being a social construct, the law (and, in our context, competition law) stems from a society's domestic values and it changes to reflect the evolution of these values. Different levels of economic development, market realities, and government and enforcement institutions can dictate differentiation in the composition of national competition provisions.

Accordingly, while all competition laws seek to protect the competitive process, enhance consumer welfare, and promote efficient markets, they may differ in the weight given to each of the goals, and in the range of other goals which form the body of law. It is not uncommon for competition law provisions to vary in different jurisdictions. Some may use the competition regime to promote a wide set of goals while others may favour a narrow application of the law—by limiting goals, or creating exemptions which exclude certain economic sectors or business practices from the application of the law.

In addition to variations in the language and scope of the law, competition law's interpretation also evolves over time. Take for example the notion of consumer welfare. While that term does not appear in US or EU legislation, it stands at the heart of antitrust enforcement. Its interpretation and scope have involved some ambiguity and have changed over time. Some have used it to argue that competition laws should protect the general welfare of society (not just that of consumers), some argue that it should include only direct purchasers, and others argue that it should encompass wide aspects of consumer wellbeing.

Different interpretations of what 'consumer welfare' encompasses result in different benchmarks against which an action is measured and considered pro-competitive or anti-competitive. More broadly, a person's understanding of the goals of competition and antitrust law will affect their views as to its desired scope.

Also relevant here are one's assumptions as to the competitiveness of markets in a given jurisdiction. As competition and antitrust laws seek to safeguard the market, one's assumption as to the inherent competitiveness of a given market may affect the implementation of the law. An underlying assumption that markets are 'naturally' competitive and would easily self-correct anti-competitive activity will likely lead to narrow interpretation of the law. A more sceptical view as to the ability of markets to self-correct may lead to a more interventionist approach.

And so, as we move beyond competition laws' 'common DNA', we encounter variation in the laws and their execution around the world. While there is an ongoing effort to align the scope of competition laws worldwide, they remain national in nature and susceptible to the forces described above. These differences result in different thresholds for illegality. Business actions which are acceptable in some jurisdictions may be deemed anti-competitive in others. Furthermore, over time, the threshold for illegality may change within each jurisdiction.

Let us illustrate these variations by looking first at the US and EU regimes and then briefly noting additional jurisdictions around the world.

United States federal antitrust laws

Enacted in 1890, the US Sherman Act provides the foundation of US federal antitrust law. The Sherman Act does not formally state the goals of the US antitrust regime; a fact which naturally led to vivid discussion, research, and political discourse on the subject.

In the regime's early years, the perceived goals of US antitrust law advanced a mix of economic, social, and political ideas which were not particularly coherent. Enforcers initially used the Sherman Act to control and restrict the economic and political power of trusts and monopolies arising from industrialization after the Civil War, giving the law its name: 'antitrust'. The Supreme Court interpreted the Sherman Act broadly to consider both economic and non-economic goals related to these monopolies. Non-economic goals included 'indirect social or moral effects', which made a system of small producers preferable, even where it caused economic inefficiencies. Interestingly, in the early days enforcers also used the Sherman Act to target victims of market power, such as labour unions and their officers.

Fast forward to the 1960s and 1970s: of note are two schools of thought which were central to the evolution of US antitrust law. In the 1960s the 'Harvard school of thought' dominated the scene with scholarship that underlined the risks stemming from market power. As the law was understood to have the goal of preventing the rise of market power, the focal point of antitrust analysis lay in the structure of the market. That scholarship led to a strict attitude towards mergers or agreements that increase market concentration and market power, regardless of their welfare effects. In the 1970s these theories gave way to the 'Chicago school of thought' which put greater trust in markets' ability to self-correct, rejected the presumption of illegality, and focused on the effects on consumer welfare. Antitrust intervention was deemed necessary only in instances where an activity was proven to undermine consumer welfare. At the time, the Chicago school of thought had led to limited enforcement actions, as most markets were deemed competitive, thus rarely requiring intervention.

Since then, as US antitrust scholarship has continued to evolve, the US courts have advanced a more nuanced approach which acknowledges the inability of some markets to self-correct and the need for effective enforcement, while still focusing on the proof of anti-competitive effects as a central pillar of antitrust enforcement. In their judgments, the US courts clarified that anti-competitive behaviour serves as the focal point of the law. The law was entrusted with the protection of competition, not competitors, and was to be implemented when harm to consumer welfare was established.

Today, policy makers continue to debate US antitrust enforcement goals. At times this debate reflects ranging viewpoints, as to the dynamics of competition, the role government should play in society, and the need for intervention.

European Union competition laws

The 1957 Treaty of Rome first established the European Economic Community's competition regime, which has evolved alongside the unique supranational entity, the EU. Current EU Competition regulation is primarily contained in the Treaty on the Functioning of the EU (TFEU) and associated legislation.

By contrast to the US Sherman Act, EU legislation provides some indication as to the goals of competition law as it positions it within the wider goals of the Union. Article 3 of the Treaty on the EU (TEU) contains a list of socio-economic objectives which the Union aims to achieve:

> The Union shall establish an internal market. It shall work for the sustainable development of Europe based on balanced economic growth and price stability, a highly competitive social market economy, aiming at full employment and social progress, and a high level of protection and improvement of the quality of the environment. It shall promote scientific and technological advance.

Competition law in the EU forms part of this matrix of values and laws aimed at maintaining the Union. The European Commission has stated: 'competition policy cannot be pursued in isolation, as an end in itself, without reference to the legal, economic, political and social context.' German ordo-liberal philosophy (which reflects humanist values protecting individual freedom from governmental and private power), and Europe's unique political reality, have greatly influenced the EU's competition regime. This regime accordingly pursues a multitude of different goals, including key objectives such as the promotion of consumer welfare and efficiency, alongside other objectives such as the protection of European market integration.

Let us elaborate on the latter. European market integration, that is, the creation of a single economic market which surpasses the boundaries between the EU member states, has been one of the major historical drivers of EU competition law. The goal of creating a single economic market is political in nature. Competition law has been assigned to advance that goal, alongside its core objectives. And so, under EU competition law, actions and agreements which re-create the boundaries between the member states may be deemed anti-competitive. While market integration is economic in nature, protecting the internal market may not always further a narrow economic concept of consumer welfare. In practice, this political goal has led to a focus on removing territorial restrictions that undermine the creation of the single market and dictates a rather restrictive view of agreements which could limit trade between member states or lead to market foreclosure.

The positioning of the competition provisions as supporting wider EU goals implies that EU competition law could take into account other policy concerns such as social protection, consumer protection, environmental concerns, and regional development. Reconciling these wider goals with the core focus on consumer welfare is not always easy.

Not surprisingly, in Europe, just like in the US, there is an ongoing lively debate on the appropriate interpretation of competition law, its goals, and its correct implementation. Some favour a narrow approach which focuses chiefly on consumer welfare, while others argue that competition law, in Europe, was mandated with broader goals and should be used to protect other values.

More than 120 jurisdictions apply competition laws

Now take the US and EU examples and multiply them again and again. With over 120 jurisdictions operating competition regimes, we have multiple versions of the same tale—each slightly differing in scope and spirit. Each uses a slightly different mechanism to achieve its goals, setting varying thresholds for illegality, exempting different sectors in the economy, and targeting others.

In China, for example, the Anti-Monopoly Law advances consumer welfare and efficiency as well as the public interest and the development of a socialist market economy. Article 15 of the Chinese Anti-Monopoly Law limits the application of the law through exemptions that apply in a range of cases: for instance, when an agreement has the purpose of reinforcing the competitiveness of small and medium-sized businesses, achieving public interests such as conserving energy, protecting the environment and relieving the victims of a disaster, mitigating serious decrease in sales volume or excessive production during economic recessions, or safeguarding interests in foreign trade or foreign economic cooperation.

In Japan, competition law promotes 'fair and free competition, to stimulate the creative initiative of entrepreneurs, to encourage business activities, to heighten the level of employment and actual national income, and thereby to promote the democratic and wholesome development of the national economy as well as to assure the interests of general consumers'. The broad language of the law was narrowed in case law, somewhat limiting its application in some instances.

In South Korea, competition law is set to encourage creative business activities, protect consumers, and promote the balanced development of the national economy by encouraging fair and free competition. In Taiwan, competition law seeks to maintain trading order, protect consumers' interests, ensure fair competition, and promote economic stability and prosperity. In Namibia, competition law serves, among other things, to protect minority empowerment. In India, Section 54 of the 2002 Competition Act creates a mechanism for exemption from the application of competition law in the interest, among other things, of security of the state or public interest. In Hong Kong,

exclusions and exemptions are listed in the Competition
Ordinance. They narrow the application of competition law in a
range of instances, including general economic interest, public
policy grounds, or in the case of statutory bodies.

The list goes on and on...

Many jurisdictions also allow for consideration of 'public interest'
which may override the application of competition law in
instances where other economic or political considerations are
deemed more important. In the UK, for instance, the secretary of
state for business and enterprise can clear a merger transaction
despite competitive concerns. That was the case, for example,
when a merger transaction between Lloyds/HBOS was approved,
as it was deemed essential to ensuring the stability of the UK's
financial system. To give another illustration, in Germany,
ministerial approval may be used to override the competition
authority decision making. That was the case, for example, when
public interest considerations led the minister for economics to
set aside a Bundeskartellamt decision to block the *E.ON/Ruhrgas*
transaction as it was deemed necessary for the stability of the
national gas supply and would have improved E.ON's
international competitiveness.

So, what is competition law about?

Competition and antitrust laws reflect our recognition of the
centrality of the competitive process to our livelihood, the need to
prevent the distortion of the competitive process and safeguard
consumer welfare. The national laws (and the political process
which underpins national legislation) are constructed to reflect
the political and social values, as well as the economic reality, in
each jurisdiction. In turn, these variations affect the interpretation
of the law and its application.

If you look beyond the inevitable national variations in the law and its interpretation, you can easily identify the common thread—competition and antitrust laws are about consumer welfare and the promotion of a free and efficient competitive process. They aim to advance a common goal—competitive markets that deliver for consumers.

Chapter 4
What is the optimal level of enforcement?

When going to the doctor to treat an illness, we receive a prescription for a medicine. It indicates clearly the dose which we should take and the duration of treatment. We appreciate the guidance. We know that taking too much of a medicine may harm us. At the same time, we understand that taking too little may not treat the illness correctly. Even worse, our condition may deteriorate and might lead to our demise.

In some ways, competition law enforcement acts like a medicine used to treat the market. Using this medicine to remedy market failures and anti-competitive activities requires skill and knowledge. If you overdo it—that is, if you over-enforce—you may harm the process of competition. Unmerited enforcement could, for example, remove the incentives of companies to compete and invest. After all, if the reward for competing fiercely against each other is a penalty, no one would compete. On the other hand, if you under-enforce—that is, you do not condemn harmful anti-competitive activities—these activities may impede the process of competition. And so, as we consider the optimal level of intervention, we aim to identify a level of enforcement that is just right. The antitrust toolbox comes with a clear warning: 'Danger!—do not over- or under-dose.'

Sometimes, the problems and solutions are clear. When faced with distinct anti-competitive activity, like a price-fixing conspiracy, competition and consumers undoubtedly suffer. The cartel is evidently illegal, and enforcers must intervene to curtail it. These 'hardcore' anti-competitive activities violate competition law.

At other times, the activity in question is not 'hardcore' and its effect on the market and consumer welfare is ambiguous. In such cases, enforcers may debate whether there is any illegality, whether competition law is the right tool for the job, and whether market forces might naturally restore competition and make intervention redundant.

Going back to our example of medicine, the challenge becomes clearer. In medicine, doctors often agree on the right dose to cure an illness, but this is not always the case in competition. Lawyers, economists, and enforcers may have different views on whether an activity is anti-competitive, and how best to address it. They may agree on the facts—that is, how a company or companies acted—but they could have different views on the action's effects and its illegality. They may disagree on the presence of an 'illness' (is there an anti-competitive activity which requires attention?), on it requiring 'medical' intervention (could the market self-correct?), on the harm any intervention could cause the 'patient' (might intervention chill competition?), and on the correct dose of 'medicine' (the legal remedy required).

Economics and law

Economic thinking serves as a key foundation and helps educate all involved on the need for intervention. It helps us to better understand a given action's effects—on competition dynamics, efficiencies, and consumer welfare—and thereby decide which cases call for intervention.

All competition jurisdictions acknowledge the central and crucial role of economic analysis in shaping competition prosecution. A primary role of economic research is to inform the general design of rules in competition law and shape their enforcement. Greater economic understanding has improved the structure of competition law through legal presumptions and thresholds, enforcement guidelines, and a greater understanding of the gravity and consequences of anti-competitive activities.

Indeed, there has been an ever-increasing 'economization' of antitrust, as more jurisdictions rely on economic analysis to determine whether intervention is needed. Economic analysis does increasingly shape the application of competition law on a case-by-case basis. Economists are often involved in all phases of the investigation and decision making. Reflecting their increasing importance, enforcement agencies allocate growing resources to ever more sophisticated teams of economists.

While undoubtedly central to competition enforcement, economic analysis has some limitations which should be acknowledged.

To begin with, the economic theory operates within the boundaries set by the law. The scope of the law affects the margin for economic analysis and the findings of economic experts do not replace legal assessment and adjudication.

Furthermore, economic analysis should not be viewed with mathematical certainty. Economic analysis is not a 'value-free science, inoculated from normative judgments'. Our choice of economic theory, economic models, and assumptions about human behaviour and market functioning, all affect the results of the economic analysis. Different choices and different assumptions may well lead to different conclusions as to the competitive effects of a given practice, and to disagreements about whether a market is dysfunctional or whether an intervention is warranted.

For example, an analysis which relies purely on neoclassical economics may lead to different outcomes than an analysis which incorporates behavioural economics. Neoclassical economics assumes that market actors are rational and aim to maximize utility. Behavioural economics acknowledges that customers are not always rational profit maximizing agents: they suffer from biases, and sellers can mislead and manipulate them. These differences in assumptions can affect our conclusion about whether conduct has anti-competitive effects.

Even where economists share the same assumptions and theories, their economic models involve necessary simplifications which render them inexact proxies for real market behaviour. From the definition of a market, through the consideration of market power, to the analysis of market dynamics and behaviour—the transition from economic theory to practice is often imprecise. Competition law, for example, traditionally defines a relevant market as a delineated space in which there is uniform competition. Commentators have long bemoaned this excessive and, at times, fictional simplicity, which doesn't accurately reflect real market behaviour. As economic modelling techniques have become more sophisticated, competition law assessment has de-emphasized market definition in favour of a focus on competitive pressures.

Returning again to our medicine example, as natural scientists, doctors can deduce with certainty how much of a medicine to prescribe from repeated randomized trials. Economists don't have the same luxury in competition cases. As one economic expert put it: 'there are few or no "universal economic truths"…Those familiar with economic theory will know that a large number of results can often be reversed by making an alternative assumption.'

The divergence in theories, assumptions, and simplifications affects one's perception of the competitive process, the relevant competition forces, one's assumptions regarding market participants, and the role of institutions in antitrust enforcement. While economic theory is crucial and vital to our understanding, it should not be treated as a neutral and value free science.

'Laissez faire'

When going to the doctor for a minor ailment such as a common cold, we sometimes receive advice that doesn't seem like medicine at all: to 'get plenty of rest' or 'drink lots of fluids'. The doctor knows that our natural immune response will fight the disease and return us to a healthy equilibrium more effectively than any treatment they could devise.

Competitive markets have similar 'self-regulating' characteristics. When markets work well, companies' attempts to act anti-competitively or abuse their market power will naturally be fleeting and unsustainable. When companies increase their prices or reduce the quality of product and services, other companies react by trying to steal their customers. The competition dynamic is self-healing, as companies compete against each other to win our business.

This suggests that when markets work well, competition enforcers are better off adopting a 'laissez-faire' approach (leaving the market to take its own course). Remedies they could prescribe are less effective than allowing the market to self-correct. Furthermore, remedies carry with them the potential to distort the market and chill natural competition. Left to their own processes, free markets will naturally develop into rich corporate ecosystems; excessive regulatory intervention will reduce them to lethargic monocultures.

Enforcers should therefore focus their attention on circumstances where competitive forces cannot self-correct the marketplace. Accordingly, intervention is called for when market failure prevents the organic dynamics of competition from dissipating possible anti-competitive effects.

But would markets easily self-correct? And how long would that process take? Would a concentrated market with a monopoly easily correct itself?

These are challenging questions. Not surprisingly, different enforcers and scholars may have varying views on the 'healing powers' of some markets and the need for intervention.

In some markets, for example, entry may be challenging and require enormous upfront investment. This would limit the ability of a potential competitor to constrain a powerful incumbent's behaviour. Knowing that, the incumbent may have the freedom and incentive to engage in anti-competitive behaviour. As the market may not easily self-correct, antitrust intervention may be called for. On the other hand, looking at the same market reality, some may argue that although entry to the market is unlikely in the short term, the threat of possible disruptive innovation is sufficient to safeguard consumer welfare.

Think for example of digital markets dominated by a powerful online platform for search, shopping, or social interactions. These markets are often characterized by network effects and high barriers to entry. They have demonstrated a tendency to 'tip' towards a particular market player, with 'winner-takes-all' or 'winner-takes-most' consequences. These platforms *become* the market for whatever segment they try to serve, with the power to set prices and quality, determine competitive parameters, and the ability to lean into neighbouring markets to create an ecosystem which their users struggle to leave. They also have the power and incentive to affect innovation paths and the money to purchase possible disruptors. Although they are undoubtedly innovative companies, it is these market dynamics that have made Google synonymous with search, Amazon with online shopping, and Facebook with social networking.

Now think of the question of competition intervention. When faced with an activity which might be objectionable on one of these markets, should the competition enforcer intervene or trust the market forces?

Some would argue that these platforms have obtained significant market power which is sustainable and supported by direct and indirect network effects, big data, and big analytics. As a market tips towards a particular platform which controls the leading ecosystem, competition is limited and market power is present. The market would therefore not easily correct itself.

Others, on the other hand, would object to this approach. First, they would argue that the market is wider. For example, Google has often argued that it competes in a wide market which spans beyond search engines and includes shopping platforms and news outlets. Second, they would argue that even if they do have a large market share, they do not benefit from market power. Competitive pressure is out there and the risk of potential competition ensures that they treat their users, input providers, and advertisers fairly. Any other strategy will quickly lead their users to use alternative platforms. Third, they would argue that even if competition is limited *in* the market, competition *for* the market still exists. Disruptive innovation is always just round the corner, and could result in a brand-new technology or business model that would undermine their market position.

If you were the competition enforcer, would you trust the digital markets to self-correct and allow the platforms freedom in operation, or would you intervene when you suspect a possible abuse of their power?

Competition enforcers have grappled with these questions in the past decade. If you trust the market, 'no action' may be the right answer. If, however, you believe the market is ill-performing, antitrust intervention may be called for. Broadly speaking, early on, while the EU had raised concerns as to the behaviour of some platforms, the US was relatively reluctant to take action, putting its trust in the markets' ability to self-correct. A good example of the disparity in approach is the EU *Google shopping* case which we will explore in detail in Chapter 9. Since then, greater consensus has emerged as to the distortion of competition in some digital markets. A significant number of reports, published in many jurisdictions (including the US, the EU, Australia, France, Germany, and the UK) and by international organizations, have suggested that an increased level of intervention is required. This has been followed by increased scrutiny in the EU, the US, and elsewhere, looking at the activities of leading platforms, including Google, Amazon, and Facebook.

Type I and Type II errors

As we have seen, the legal provisions—the letter of the law—offer flexibility in application. Economic analysis can help guide enforcers as to the optimal level of enforcement, but economics is not a value free science. It cannot always conclusively determine whether intervention is merited (will the market self-correct?), what is legal, or what should be condemned. Hence, some uncertainty is inevitable when enforcing competition law.

Between activities that are clearly anti-competitive (like cartels, which will be discussed in Chapter 7) and activities that are clearly pro-competitive lies a vast grey horizon. Here, multiple outcomes to an inquiry are possible.

As we noted above, key here is one's belief as to the dynamism of the market and its ability to self-correct. After all, if one trusts that the invisible hand of competition has the capacity to overcome market failures and restore competition, intervention may be deemed superfluous.

Let us now add another dimension, that of error costs: the costs associated with either over- or under-intervention.

A *Type I error*, known as a false positive, refers to instances in which competition law was unnecessarily applied. This unnecessary application risks chilling and distorting the competitive process. Clearly, competition enforcers try to avoid this type of error as it amounts to an over-dosing on the competition medicine, using enforcement in instances where it is not necessary.

A *Type II error*, known as a false negative, refers to a situation when the law was not applied where it should have been. Under-enforcement of competition law leads to a failure to correct a market distortion which continues to harm consumers. Again, competition enforcers try hard to avoid this type of error as it amounts to an under-dosing on the competition medicine, failing to intervene when needed.

Ideally, one would try to avoid both error costs, but that is easier said than done. Often it is hard to know whether to intervene and what remedy is best suited to resolve the competitive problem. Lawyers, economists, and other experts often spend hours arguing both sides. The optimal enforcement action is not always easy to identify.

With this uncertainty in mind, which error would be less costly? Would you rather over-dose or under-dose?

Here we go back to our trust in the market dynamic. If one believes that market forces would self-correct, then under-enforcement may carry less risk, as the market forces could potentially remedy the problem. Accordingly, when in doubt, it would be safer to limit antitrust intervention. If, on the other hand, one puts less faith in the market's ability to self-correct, under-enforcement, at the very least, carries the same cost as over-enforcement.

Our approach to error costs not only affects the decision to intervene in a given case, it also affects the legal process—for example, the level of proof required to establish antitrust violation. A standard of proof that is too high will result in few successful cases and a limited impact. A standard of proof too low will result in unsubstantiated findings of antitrust violations when none exist.

As a society we very much strive to get it right and set the level of intervention at the optimal level. So, who decides?

Beyond the written letter of the law, many people constantly affect the scope and intensity of competition enforcement: the judges who hear competition cases and appeals; the enforcers who decide which cases to pursue; market players who may sue others for anti-competitive activities; the economists who provide analyses of the likely effects of enforcement; the lawyers who interpret and shape the legal rules; and the companies operating on the market, which often invest heavily in lobbying and promoting discussion that serves their commercial interests.

Together, all of these actors affect the competition culture and appetite for intervention in each jurisdiction. They affect the way competition is taught at a given time and at a given university, and the public perception of right and wrong. At times, all will agree; at other times, variations will emerge within and between jurisdictions.

Chapter 5
The legal framework

Having explored the policy and theory which affects antitrust intervention, let us now briefly outline the key competition provisions in the US and the EU.

Like in most other jurisdictions, EU and US laws include competition provisions that are used to address antitrust violations such as anti-competitive agreements or abuse of monopoly power, as well as laws dealing with proposed mergers and acquisitions.

Let us elaborate on these provisions.

US antitrust law—anti-competitive agreements

Section 1 of the Sherman Antitrust Act prohibits contracts and agreements between two or more individuals or entities in restraint of trade or commerce. Infringement of the Section may result in the imposition of a fine on individuals or entities and may also lead to imprisonment of individuals who were involved in blatant hardcore infringements.

The consideration of violations of Section 1 may be carried out using one of two standards: the *rule of reason* or the *'per-se' approach*.

The rule of reason standard requires a detailed analysis of the market reality and the possible harmful and competitive effects of the activity or agreement in question. The US Supreme Court first articulated the rule in *Board of Trade of Chicago v United States*:

> The true test of legality is whether the restraint imposed is such as merely regulates, and perhaps thereby promotes competition, or whether it is such as may suppress or even destroy competition. To determine that question the court must ordinarily consider the facts peculiar to the business to which the restraint is applied, its condition before and after the restraint is imposed, the nature of the restraint, and its effect, actual or probable.

In *Leegin Creative Leather Products, Inc. v PSKS, Inc.* the US Supreme Court elaborated on the scope of the requisite analysis. The court noted that the doctrine 'distinguishes between restraints with anti-competitive effect that are harmful to the consumer and restraints stimulating competition that are in the consumer's best interest.' The analysis requires one to weigh all of the relevant circumstances including information about the relevant business and its market power, the restraint's history, source, nature, its usage by other companies, and its overall effect.

To establish a violation under the rule of reason standard, the plaintiff must establish an anti-competitive effect on a given market within a given geographic area, and demonstrate injury or imminent threat of injury to its business (as a threshold matter, the plaintiff must show that the defendant has market power capable of causing anti-competitive effects). If successful, the burden then shifts to the defendant to show 'pro-competitive justification', for example, promoting inter-brand competition, enhancing efficiency, or market innovation.

By contrast to the rule of reason, the *per-se* rule will apply in instances where there is clear and blatant infringement of the law. This will be the case, for example, when the restraint in question involves price fixing, bid rigging, market sharing, or other violations that would always (or almost always) tend to restrict competition and decrease output. In such cases, the practice will be deemed to infringe the law and there will be no need for any inquiry into the market context in which the restraint operates, consideration of its effect, or the existence of an objective competitive justification.

To establish a violation under the *per-se* rule, the plaintiff will need to provide evidence of the activity, but there is no need to demonstrate the anti-competitive effect of the restraint. The defendant cannot justify the infringement by providing an objective competitive justification.

In addition to the rule of reason and the *per-se* rule, a third framework for analysis may be used at times. This is known as the 'quick-look' analysis, which is used where the *per-se* framework is inappropriate but there is no need for a full-blown rule of reason analysis. In *Agnew v National Collegiate Athletic Association*, the US Court of Appeal explained that the quick-look approach can be used when the arrangements in question would have an anti-competitive effect on customers and markets, but where there still remain reasons to examine potential pro-competitive justifications.

In Chapters 7 and 8 we will explore the application of this Section to different types of agreements.

US antitrust law—abuse of market power

Section 2 of the Sherman Antitrust Act makes it illegal for individuals or entities to monopolize or attempt to monopolize any area of trade or commerce. The Section does not condemn market power as such but rather its wilful acquisition or maintenance. The term 'wilfully' refers to improper conduct that excludes or drives rivals from the market on some basis other than competition merits.

In *US v E.I. Du Pont de Nemours & Co*, the Supreme Court defined monopoly power as 'the power to control prices or exclude competition'. Usually, monopoly power is inferred from a firm's possession of a dominant share of a market characterized by barriers to entry.

To establish monopolization under Section 2 the plaintiff must prove that the defendant possesses monopoly power in a relevant market and that it was acquired or maintained wilfully, instead of through organic growth or development as a consequence of a superior product, business acumen, or even historic accident. The offence of attempted monopolization requires proof of a dangerous probability, specific intent to monopolize a particular market, and anti-competitive behaviour.

In *Spectrum Sports, Inc. v McQuillan*, the Supreme Court noted that courts have been careful to avoid liberal application of Section 2 in a way that may chill competition. The court clarified that

> [t]he purpose of the Act is not to protect businesses from the working of the market; it is to protect the public from the failure of the market. The law directs itself not against conduct which is competitive, even severely so, but against conduct which unfairly tends to destroy competition itself.

In Chapter 9, we will consider the application of Section 2 in more detail.

EU competition law—anti-competitive agreements

Article 101 of the TFEU prohibits agreements between 'undertakings' (individuals and entities that engage in economic activity) that have as their object or effect the prevention, restriction, or distortion of competition, and affect trade between the EU member states.

An anti-competitive object and anti-competitive effects constitute alternative conditions, and are distinguishable by the fact that certain forms of collusion between entities—such as price fixing and market sharing—can 'be regarded, by their very nature, as being injurious to the proper functioning of normal competition'. In such instances where the agreement reveals 'a sufficient degree of harm to competition' making the anti-competitive object apparent, there is no need to take account of the concrete effect of the agreement in question.

While similar to the US *'per-se'* approach, the EU analysis of the 'object' differs in that it is context-dependent and may be affected by the market reality. Furthermore, parties may raise defence arguments under Article 101(3) TFEU and could, in principle, show that the restriction of competition is exempt from the scope of the law (we will elaborate on Article 101(3) further below).

When an agreement does not have the object of restricting competition, its effect should be considered. In *Société Technique Minière v Maschinenbau Ulm GmbH*, the court outlined the nature of the inquiry, which involved a review of the agreement or communication within the actual context in which it occurred, in order to conclude that competition had in fact been prevented, restricted, or distorted to an appreciable extent. Assessment of effects was based on a thorough analysis of the economic and legal context in which the agreements at issue occurred and the specificities of the relevant market.

Agreements that are found to infringe Article 101(1) TFEU, by their object or by their effect, may nonetheless be exempted under Article 101(3) TFEU when they contribute to improving the production or distribution of goods, or to the promotion of technical or economic progress while allowing consumers a fair share of the benefit; and do not impose restrictions which are not indispensable to the attainment of these objectives, or eliminate competition in respect of a substantial part of the products in question. The Article may apply to individual cases and has also been used to establish general block exemptions which exempt certain categories of agreement.

In Chapters 7 and 8 we will explore in more detail the application of Article 101 TFEU to different types of agreements.

EU competition law—abuse of market power

Article 102 TFEU condemns the abuse, by one or more entities, of a dominant position within the internal market when that abuse affects trade between EU member states. Article 102 TFEU does not prevent companies and other entities from acquiring, on their own merits, a dominant position in a market. The Article only condemns the abuse of a dominant position.

One would first need to define the relevant market and then establish that the company in question holds a position of power on that market. In *Hoffmann-La Roche & Co. v Commission,* the European Court of Justice held that a dominant position is one which enables the company 'to prevent effective competition being maintained on the relevant market by affording it the power to behave to an appreciable extent independently of its competitors, its customers and ultimately of the consumers'.

Once dominance has been established, one needs to consider whether it has been abused. Article 102 TFEU outlines a non-exhaustive list of possible actions which may amount to an abuse of market power. The Court of Justice has clarified that Article 102 TFEU applies not only to practices which may cause damage to consumers directly (through exploitation), but also to those which are detrimental to them through their impact on competition dynamics (through exclusion of other as-efficient competitors from the market).

In Chapter 9, we will consider in more detail the application of Article 102 TFEU and abuse of market power.

Merger control

Another important area of competition enforcement is *merger control*. The US and the EU have special laws that address proposed merger transactions and other types of acquisitions, and enable the competition agencies to review them and ensure that they will not significantly lessen competition in the relevant market.

Merger review in the EU and the US differs from antitrust enforcement under the provisions discussed earlier, not least as it is conducted before the transaction takes place. It involves a prospective analysis of proposed transactions and their predicted impact on the market. We will elaborate on this in Chapter 10.

Chapter 6
Who enforces the law?

So far, we have understood the goals of the law and the importance of measured intervention. We are now also aware of the key antitrust provisions. But who enforces them?

In most countries, competition and antitrust laws can be utilized by the public enforcer (the competition agency) that is tasked with maintaining a competitive environment; or by private entities (companies, individuals, and organizations) that use the competition provisions to protect their commercial interests or claim damages for loss caused by violation of competition law.

We distinguish between these two types of enforcement, referring to one as *public* enforcement and the other as *private* enforcement.

Public enforcement of competition law

'Public enforcement' refers to enforcement of the law by the state, through a dedicated enforcer.

Here the public agency investigates an alleged infringement of the law and brings it to an end, much as the police will take action when faced with a crime. Public enforcement allows the state to shape competition policy and consider public interest as a whole while carrying out its mission to safeguard markets and consumer welfare.

Investigations of alleged infringements could start on the agency's own initiative, when it suspects foul play or is worried about the level of competition in a given market. Sometimes an investigation will start following a complaint by a customer or competitor. At other times, it may start following a tipoff by one of the parties to an anti-competitive agreement.

Once the agency decides to take up a case, it will analyse the market, the legality of the behaviour, and its impact on competition. If infringement of the law is established, the agency will press ahead with the case with an aim of imposing remedies to restore competition. The agency may also seek to punish the violator by imposing a fine and sometimes even personal sanctions on individuals, including imprisonment.

Competition agencies often benefit from extensive enforcement powers that enable them to discharge their responsibilities effectively. They can gather information, interview suspects, gain access to sensitive commercial information outside the public domain, and search the premises of suspected violators. As part of an investigation, agencies can issue binding orders for entities to provide information (at times they will require the help of the court to execute some of these powers).

Let us briefly review public enforcement in the US and the EU.

Public enforcement of US antitrust law

Federal enforcement

In the US, at the federal level, two agencies share responsibility for competition enforcement: the Federal Trade Commission's Bureau of Competition and the Antitrust Division of the Department of Justice (DOJ).

Broadly speaking, both the DOJ and FTC can pursue civil antitrust cases under Section 1 or Section 2 of the Sherman Antitrust Act. One key difference is that in its actions, the FTC will rely on the FTC Act which empowers its action. As a result, civil cases brought by the FTC would be alleged violations of Section 5 of the FTC Act. The FTC Act was not enacted to merely duplicate the scope of the Sherman Antitrust Act but was in fact designed to 'supplement and bolster the Sherman Act'. It empowers the FTC to prevent unfair methods of competition and unfair or deceptive acts or practices. To date, the FTC has made limited use of this extended mandate in competition cases. Renewed public interest in the scope of antitrust has reinvigorated debates about the FTC's use of this power.

The FTC and DOJ share responsibility for civil antitrust enforcement, but in practice they tend to divide the workload based on their industry experience: the FTC focuses on consumer-facing industries such as healthcare, food, energy, and technology; while the DOJ handles cases in telecommunications, financial services, railroads, and airlines. As part of their joint effort, the agencies coordinate their actions to avoid duplicative efforts. Their collaboration extends also to the issuing of joint guidelines on their enforcement priorities and substantive approach.

As for criminal enforcement of antitrust law, that authority is reserved to the DOJ, which can bring cases involving criminal penalties. Criminal antitrust sanctions differ from civil sanctions in that they generally involve higher fines, jail time for company executives, and collateral legal consequences arising from a criminal conviction. The DOJ will seek criminal sanctions in cases that involve explicitly anti-competitive agreements between horizontal competitors where the parties know their agreements have anti-competitive effects (such as price fixing, bid rigging, and dividing a market).

State enforcement

US state attorney generals can also enforce federal antitrust laws on behalf of their citizens. Their interest in bringing antitrust cases has changed over the years, and courts have occasionally restricted their powers to bring federal antitrust cases. Since the 1980s, states have taken a more active role in antitrust enforcement, in response to more relaxed federal enforcement since the Reagan administration.

Almost all US states, as well as the District of Columbia, have adopted their own state antitrust laws. These laws are generally pegged to federal antitrust laws, but states occasionally apply less demanding tests for certain infringements, leading to a divergence in federal and state standards.

Today, states see themselves as equal to federal enforcers in antitrust proceedings and pursue their own enforcement agendas (whether under federal or state law). The FTC and DOJ have made efforts to converge state and federal enforcement priorities, and there are synergies where states pursue cases with more local market knowledge. But states still diverge in some areas: they are more likely to challenge mergers and resale price maintenance cases, for example.

Public enforcement of European competition law

Enforcement by the EU

As in the US, competition law in the EU operates at both the EU level and at the member state level. EU law grants the European Commission primary responsibility for enforcing EU competition laws: Commission decisions create precedents which national authorities and courts must follow.

The Commission has the power to find an infringement of competition law and impose behavioural or structural remedies to bring the infringement to an end. Behavioural remedies involve ordering the infringing parties to change their behaviour in some way, normally by ceasing to engage in conduct which infringes competition law. Structural remedies affect the infringing parties' assets, for example by being required to dispose of a minority shareholding, dissolve a joint venture, or break up an entity. The Commission will generally only apply structural remedies if behavioural remedies are not sufficient to stop an infringement.

The Commission can also accept commitments from entities subject to investigation to bring a competition law infringement to an end. (A similar mechanism of voluntary compliance by entering into a consent order is also available under US law.) The Commission uses this tool frequently, generally in less serious cases where it plans to bring a decision to find a violation but the entities concerned voluntarily offer to change their behaviour. Entities offering such commitments avoid a formal decision that would have found a violation of competition law, and the Commission can turn to focus its resources on more serious infringements.

A key difference between EU and US public enforcement lies in the role of the court. In the EU, the European Commission investigates the violation and reaches a decision as to the legality of the action and the appropriate remedy. While no court order is required, parties may appeal against the Commission's decision and apply to the General Court asking for its annulment. On appeal, the court will consider whether the Commission erred in its analysis, but it will not consider the case *de novo* (meaning the court does not hear and consider again the original arguments and evidence). In the US, on the other hand, the agencies would generally go to court to prove their case. The court will hear the case and counter-arguments by the parties before issuing its ruling. The court decision can then be appealed by the parties.

Enforcement by EU member states

Like in the US, European member states will have their own public enforcers of competition law—competition agencies that are able to enforce the European competition provisions. When they do so, their enforcement powers are broadly similar to those of the European Commission.

The national competition agencies of the member states can also apply national competition law, which in most cases is similar to the European provisions.

While EU competition law does not carry criminal sanctions, some EU member states have adopted criminal sanctions in national law for serious competition law infringements.

Private competition law enforcement

Private parties affected by anti-competitive conduct can often bring a civil action in court against those responsible for violating competition law. At times, private parties will seek injunctive relief to force those engaging in anti-competitive conduct to end their illegal activity. Often, private parties seek damages as compensation for the harms caused by anti-competitive activity.

Two categories of private enforcement damages actions are worthy of note.

The first category involves *'follow-on' damages actions*, which follow a finding of competition law infringement in a case brought by a public enforcer. These actions use the public enforcer's decision to support their claim for compensation in court. By doing so, private parties overcome part of the risk and cost of litigating a competition case. This makes follow-on actions popular among private litigants.

The second category concerns *'stand-alone' damages actions*. These actions are more complex as the claimant must prove, not only that a competition law violation harmed the claimant, but also that the defendant in question violated competition law. These actions are understandably less common, due to their greater risk and cost, and the difficulty a private party has in obtaining adequate information to substantiate its claim. Stand-alone actions have particular public value because they help antitrust enforcers discover problems and augment their casework with private resources.

While private damages actions are meant to compensate the individual or company which suffered harm due to the anti-competitive activity, they also have an important public function. The private litigants act as enforcers of competition law and help foster a competitive culture. Their actions help unravel competition violations (stand-alone claims) as well as increasing deterrence (stand-alone and follow-on claims). This public value of private actions has led governments to encourage these forms of litigation.

Noteworthy, in particular, is the approach taken in the US. To encourage private actions, the US gives private parties the right to claim treble damages for harms which arise from antitrust infringements. This incentive, combined with more permissive rules in bringing class actions, has created a much more active private enforcement landscape in the US than in other jurisdictions. While this approach stimulates private enforcement, it may, at times, result in over-deterrence, encouraging frivolous lawsuits, and providing windfalls and weapons to competitors who wish to use litigation for commercial advantage.

Private parties' pursuit of competition actions through the courts plays an important role in competition law's overall enforcement.

It supplements public enforcement of competition law and enhances its deterrent effect. By harnessing a private party's economic interests to ensure the full effectiveness of competition rules, private enforcement plays an important role in sustaining a competitive economy. Furthermore, private enforcement promotes parties' individual rights by providing them a channel for corrective justice through compensation and injunctive relief. In doing so, it complements the public system and safeguards the rights of private individuals in their relations with one another.

Chapter 7
The fight against cartels

As we illustrated in Chapter 1, in a competitive market companies strive to outperform each other. They try to win the competitive process by lowering prices and improving the quality of goods and services. Competitive markets, while beneficial to consumers, force businesses to work hard—they need to continuously invest in service and quality and strive to improve their efficiency. Only by being better than others can they sell larger quantities (often at lower prices) and increase profitability.

Faced with competitive pressure, some companies may seek respite by trying to undermine the process of competition. Rather than compete against each other on price, quality, and service, they may secretly agree among themselves to do the opposite. This would dampen competition by fixing the price of products and services, and dividing the market or allocating customers between them. These illegal agreements to restrict competition (and harm consumers) are generally referred to as 'cartel agreements'.

A typical cartel will take place in a market which is relatively concentrated with a handful of leading sellers. The sellers' products will be of similar type and quality, which makes it easier for them to agree on a common strategy. The sellers in question may secretly meet or communicate in order to limit the competition between them.

The customers, unaware of the secret cartel agreement, confront a marketplace with higher prices, and assume these prices are competitive. After all, a competitive market could produce uniform prices for a given product, just as a price-fixing conspiracy could. Absent the benefits of the competitive process, the cartel members extract their customers' surplus of wealth (the money we would have saved had there been proper competition in the marketplace).

When unchallenged and undetected, cartel activity can distort competition and significantly harm consumer welfare and trade. Policy makers have described cartel activity as a cancer in a modern market economy, the effects of which are entirely negative. The law reflects this view by treating cartel activity as unambiguously bad, and thus prescribing harsh penalties to violators. Competition agencies position these illicit activities high on their enforcement agenda.

Illegality

Cartel activity—which involves price fixing, bid rigging, customer allocation, or market sharing (activities which clearly harm the competitive process)—is regarded as a hardcore, *per-se* violation of competition laws.

In the US, Section 1 of the Sherman Antitrust Act prohibits anti-competitive contracts, combinations, or conspiracies in restraint of trade. The approach to cartel activity is harsh and uncompromising. Hardcore violations, such as price fixing, bid rigging, or market sharing, are considered so harmful to the competitive process that they are deemed '*per-se*' violations of the Act. They will almost always be deemed illegal, regardless of the specific market context, or possible justifications or defences raised by the infringing parties.

In the EU, Article 101 TFEU prohibits agreements and concerted practices that have as their object or effect the prevention or restriction of competition. Similar to the US, cartel activity—which may include price fixing, market sharing, or bid rigging—amounts to a clear violation of competition laws and will almost always be deemed to have the object of restricting competition.

Effective enforcement

For law abiding citizens, the knowledge that an action is illegal would usually suffice to deter a violation of the law. Others, however, among them cartel members, are likely to pay little regard to the law and its clear prohibitions, unless they fear punishment for their actions. This is why credible deterrence is crucial to ensure effective enforcement against cartels.

But how do you ensure that a particular level of deterrence is adequate?

The competition agency needs to establish an effective enforcement regime that will significantly increase the risk of punishment for cartel members, so much so that they will refrain from illegal activity in fear of the likely consequences. The effectiveness of the enforcement regime depends on two key variables: the first is the likelihood of detection; and the second, the level and severity of the penalty.

> Likelihood of detection x Penalty = Level of deterrence

Deficiencies at either level (detection or penalty) will likely undermine the deterrent effect and result in continued anti-competitive activity.

Let us illustrate with a simple example: If entering into an illegal cartel would result in a benefit of $100 and the penalty for that crime is $200, would a rational culprit engage in the illegal activity?

Looking at the deterrence equation above, it becomes clear that much will depend on the likelihood of detection. If the chance of the competition agency detecting the cartel is only 10 per cent, a rational offender would find the crime profitable.

> 10% x $200 = $20 (which is lower than the benefit of $100)

And so, in order for the enforcement regime to be effective, the competition agency will need, in our example, to increase the likelihood of detection to above 50 per cent (which would result in an average penalty higher than the expected gain). Alternatively, if detection is difficult and remains at 10 per cent likelihood, the agency will need to increase the level of penalty to above $1,000.

The fight against cartels depends on high penalties and detection rates. Let us consider the means by which competition agencies address these elements.

Corporate fines and damage claims

The competition laws in the US, the EU, and elsewhere enable the agencies to impose hefty fines on companies involved in the cartel activity.

In the US, following prosecution by the DOJ, corporations may be subjected to penalties of up to $100 million, or twice the cartel's gain or consumers' loss (whichever is greater). For example, in April 2020, the DOJ fined Florida Cancer Specialists $100 million for agreeing with another oncology provider to share their market for cancer patients in southern Florida.

In the EU, the European Commission can impose hefty fines on the companies involved, of up to 10 per cent of their turnover. For example, in its Truck cartel investigation (2016) the EU Commission imposed a fine of €2.9 billion on five of Europe's biggest truck makers that took part in cartel activity. In its Forex cartel investigation (2019) the Commission fined five banks €1.07 billion for participating in a foreign exchange spot trading cartel.

In addition to fines imposed on the corporations, cartel members may be ordered to pay damages to those who have suffered from the cartel activity. It is often the case that a follow-on damage claim results in cartel members being required to pay compensation for damage they inflicted on consumers.

While high financial penalties (fines and damage claims) imposed on the corporate entity may enhance the deterrence effect, we should acknowledge their limitations. First, at times, the benefit from the cartel activity may outweigh the fine. Second, financial penalties may lose some of their bite when they apply to the corporation and not the individuals who instigated the cartel activity. When individuals remain shielded from the fine (which applies to the company and not to them), they externalize much of the cost and risk associated with the illegal activity. This often gives rise to an 'agency problem' as these individuals only partially internalize the associated cost, yet they reap the gains from the illegal activity. The cost of the fine or damages claim is felt instead by the corporation, its shareholders, or even at times its customers.

Sanctions on individuals—imprisonment, fines, and disqualifications

The 'agency problem' draws attention to individual accountability as a decisive instrument to ensure effective cartel enforcement. Many competition regimes around the world therefore supplement corporate fines with individual sanctions imposed on directors and managers of the company that was involved in cartel activity.

Imprisonment

Key to effective deterrence is the threat of imprisonment, which can help bring home the message that those individuals involved in cartel activity will pay a *personal* price for their involvement. The threat of custodial sentencing focuses the attention of company managers on the personal consequences of participating in cartels. By targeting individuals within corporations, it may create a rift between them thus further destabilizing the cartel agreement. Leading the way is the US, where individuals who participated in cartel activity may be imprisoned for up to 10 years. By contrast, EU competition law does not include a criminal sanction and is administrative in nature. However, individuals may be imprisoned under the criminal laws of some EU member states.

Individual fines

In the US, following prosecution, individuals may be fined up to $1 million under the Sherman Act. Even higher individual fines may be imposed under the *Alternative Fines Act*. By contrast, EU competition law, being administrative in nature, only applies to companies or entities engaged in economic activity. It does not penalize individuals who participate in a cartel. Some EU member states have the power to impose penalties on individuals under their national laws.

Other individual sanctions

Some jurisdictions provide for other individual sanctions, such as disqualification orders. Note for example the UK Directors Disqualification Act, which can prevent a director who infringed the competition provisions from serving in directorship roles for up to 15 years after the enforcement action. Director disqualification remedies are gaining popularity globally as an effective way to deter anti-competitive conduct, and have been adopted in many jurisdictions.

Increased detection—leniency programmes

Cartel members, knowing that their illegal actions are high on the enforcement agenda of competition agencies, invest efforts and resources into concealing their activities. They are often very careful in their communications, meet in secret locations, and work hard to outsmart the competition agencies. The task of unravelling a cartel conspiracy is therefore challenging.

To increase the likelihood of detection, competition agencies take steps to destabilize cartels by putting in place leniency programmes which incentivize cartel members to approach the agency and confess their participation. Leniency programmes tap into any distrust among cartel members, and offer an immunity from prosecution and prison sentences, or reduction in fines, to the first cartel member to confess and offer information which will incriminate the other members of the cartel.

The reward system is designed to create distrust among cartel members, as they fear that others may seek immunity or a reduction in fines. Leniency programmes present each cartel member with a dilemma as to whether to trust the other cartel members. If one company, being a member of the cartel, suspects another cartel member may approach the agency for leniency, then that company would want to move faster and apply for leniency first. Other cartel members face a similar prisoner's dilemma, and would also aim to secure immunity first.

Leniency programmes have had a significant effect on cartel enforcement and are considered one of the key instruments for exposing cartels. They offer immunity for both corporate and individual cartel members, incentivizing anyone involved to consider self-reporting the activity.

While in theory, immunity programmes would make it irrational to even enter a cartel agreement, the reality is less impressive. In practice, cartel members often put in place mechanisms to circumvent effective detection and law enforcement. Furthermore, difficulties in risk assessment, over-confidence biases, or doubts as to the true benefits of leniency applications can lead some cartel members to take the risk and continue their illegal activity.

It is hard to assess the true impact of leniency programmes. We know that they help uncover many cartels, but might these exposed cartels only form the tip of the iceberg? A conservative estimation would suggest that for every cartel we uncover, there are likely to be several that remain undetected.

Increased detection—dawn raids, monitoring, and complaints

The enforcement toolbox available to competition agencies goes beyond leniency programmes. You may have come across news stories on competition agencies raiding the offices of companies in search of evidence and documents. These surprise searches, commonly referred to as 'dawn raids', enable competition agencies to obtain evidence of cartel activity or other competition law violations. They often involve both physical searching through documents and advanced screening of digital media, computers, and servers.

In addition to powers to search the premises of suspected companies, many competition agencies also operate market monitoring teams, which are tasked to review the way businesses operate in some markets, and to assesses whether their activities, cross-payments, or lack of competition suggest the presence of illicit cartels.

Every agency will encourage anyone who believes they are affected by cartel activity to complain to the agency. Some agencies also

offer financial rewards for information about cartel activity that
could lead to prosecution.

The Air Cargo Cartel

To demonstrate the uncompromising fight against cartels, let us
review one conspiracy about air cargo charges which both the US
and the EU investigated.

Our global economy is based on our ability to competitively
import and export goods, and to deliver them in the most efficient
manner to customers around the world. But what happens if one
part in this machine does not deliver on the competitive promise?
If, for example, airfreight operators decide to dampen competition
by entering into a cartel activity to increase prices for their
service?

The answer is clear—the formation of such a cartel will result in
higher prices for imported goods and in consumers paying more
but getting less. Such price-fixing conspiracy transfers money
from our pockets to those of the greedy cartel members. And that
is exactly what happened some years ago, with a large number
of airfreight operators engaging in an illegal cartel. The cartel
included leading companies such as Air Canada, Air France/KLM,
British Airways, Cathay Pacific, Japan Airlines, LAN Chile,
Qantas, SAS, Singapore Airlines, and Lufthansa.

How did we learn about the cartel? The cartel operated from
December 1999 to February 2006. In 2005, one of the cartel
members (Lufthansa) had a change of heart and decided to apply
for leniency with the aim of obtaining immunity from fines.

Following leniency applications in the US, the EU, and other
jurisdictions (including South Africa, Australia, New Zealand, and
Germany), the EU Commission and the US DOJ each opened an
investigation into the price-fixing conspiracy. In February 2006,

they launched coordinated dawn raids on the offices of several of the cartel members.

Both agencies concluded that the airlines' cartel clearly infringed competition law. By agreeing to fixed surcharges and other price components for air cargo, the cartel members had reduced the pressure of competition in the market for airfreight services. This direct fixing of prices represented a 'hardcore' violation of competition rules, as the very purpose of the agreement was to increase prices and profits for the cartel members. As the European Commission noted in its decision:

> [T]he addressees have coordinated their pricing behavior amounting to price fixing which is prohibited by Article 101 of the TFEU. Article 101 expressly includes as restrictive of competition agreements and concerted practices which directly or indirectly fix selling prices or any other trading conditions … Price being the main instrument of competition, arrangements between competitors directed at the coordination of their behavior in order to remove uncertainty in the market in respect of pricing matters … will by their very nature prevent, restrict or distort competition within the meaning of Article 101(1) of the TFEU.

What was the penalty? In the US, enforcers imposed more than $1.8 billion in criminal fines on members of the cartel. In addition, eight executives were sentenced to serve prison time due to their participation in the cartel activity. One of the executives, a European national, evaded justice for a decade, hiding from the authorities. The long arm of the law triumphed at last in January 2020 when she was apprehended in Italy and extradited to the US. She was subsequently sentenced to 14 months in a US prison.

US Assistant Attorney General Makan Delrahim of the DOJ's Antitrust Division, commented on the sentencing, saying: 'The Antitrust Division and its partners are committed to rooting out international price-fixing cartels that cheat American consumers and producers.'

In Europe, the Commission (in a decision which was re-adopted in 2017) fined the air cargo carriers €776 million for the price-fixing cartel. The commissioner in charge of competition policy, Margrethe Vestager, said in a public statement:

> Millions of businesses depend on air cargo services, which carry more than 20% of all EU imports and nearly 30% of EU exports. Working together in a cartel rather than competing to offer better services to customers does not fly with the Commission. Today's decision ensures that companies that were part of the air cargo cartel are sanctioned for their behavior.

Additional fines were also imposed on cartel members by other competition agencies, including the Australian and Canadian agencies, which investigated the price-fixing conspiracy. Cartel members were further subjected to damages claims launched by companies that suffered losses, having purchased air cargo services at inflated prices.

This case illustrates the uncompromising attitude towards hardcore restrictions to competition, and the collaboration between competition agencies in seeking to punish cartel members.

Chapter 8
Horizontal and vertical agreements

Cartel activity, as described in Chapter 7, is unambiguously anti-competitive and illegal. As a society, we aim to eliminate such illicit interactions between companies, as they result in clearly adverse effects on consumers and markets. But not all communications and interactions between companies are anti-competitive and illegal. In fact, many times companies have to interact with each other in order to engage in legitimate business activity. Open communications and exchanges of ideas and information between companies are a daily occurrence. Often, they are meant to facilitate legitimate goals such as improving production, distribution, research, and trade.

Looking at the various communications and agreements between companies, it is helpful to note three key points on the spectrum of illegality. On one end we have agreements that raise 'no competitive concerns'. In such instances an agreement between companies will have no restrictions or adverse effects on competition. On the other end are communications and cartel agreements which are manifestly anti-competitive, and include clear and harmful restrictions. Here, as illustrated in Chapter 6, the '*per-se*' and 'object' approaches will apply, and illegality is assumed. In the middle are agreements that arise from presumably legitimate business interaction but include some restrictions on competition that could give rise to anti-competitive effects.

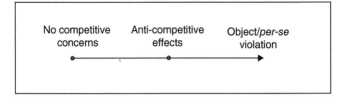

No competitive concerns   Anti-competitive effects   Object/*per-se* violation

In this chapter we look at this middle point—agreements and communications which may give rise to anti-competitive effects. There is no assumption of illegality which applies to these agreements (no '*per-se*' nor 'object' assumption), and agencies are required to consider their effects in a given market context.

To do so, agencies need to identify a relevant market (see the discussion in Chapter 2 on market definition) and consider its characteristics. The market provides much-needed context to the analysis, and enables the agencies to evaluate pro-competitive and possible anti-competitive effects.

The law

As outlined in Chapter 5, in the US, the effects-based analysis is referred to as the *rule of reason*, which is used to consider possible anti-competitive effects that are harmful to the consumer and possible benefits that stimulate competition and are in the consumer's best interest. Accordingly, the analysis will encompass a complete review of the benefits and drawbacks of an agreement within the market context.

Similarly, under EU law, the examination of effects will include consideration of the market reality, the conditions of competition, the economic context in which the companies operate, and the products or services concerned. By contrast to the US rule of reason approach, the EU Article 101 TFEU adopts a two-stage analysis. Under Article 101(1) TFEU, the effects of the agreement in its market context are explored. If an anti-competitive effect is established under Article 101(1) TFEU, the burden of proof shifts to the defendant who can then show, using Article 101(3) TFEU, that the agreement in question is nonetheless beneficial.

Having reminded ourselves of the legal provisions, we'll consider their application to horizontal and vertical agreements.

Horizontal agreements

Horizontal collaborations and agreements take place between companies at the same level of manufacturing, distribution, or retail. For example, a collaboration between several car manufacturers or an agreement between two or more supermarkets.

These agreements may be commercially attractive and pro-competitive when they enable companies to engage in joint research and development, exchanges of know-how, standard setting, cost savings, and risk mitigation. It is therefore not uncommon for companies that operate on the same market to try to improve their performance through horizontal cooperation. At times, however, while the agreement in question may have a legitimate purpose, some of its provisions may have the effect of limiting competition. A horizontal cooperation agreement may include restrictions on companies' freedom to compete on their operation, or may include provisions which facilitate exchange of sensitive information. A nuanced analysis is called for. This is illustrated in the treatment of information exchange agreements.

Information exchange between competitors

Information flows play a central role in facilitating competitive markets. After all, for the powers of competition to work, buyers require information about products, prices, and quality. Sellers benefit from legitimate information exchange about new products, technologies, standards, and market trends. Without information and sufficient market transparency, competition will under-perform. On the other hand, exchange of information could have an adverse effect when it removes some of the uncertainty inherent to the competitive process. By exchanging 'too much' or 'too sensitive' information, companies may dampen the competitive process and remove the incentives to compete.

Since information exchange may generate both pro-competitive and anti-competitive results, its analysis calls for a review of its effects in a given case. Such analysis will likely take into account the market characteristics (is it a concentrated market? How many companies operate in the market?), the level of transparency achieved through the exchange of information (to what extent does it undermine the uncertainty which is a condition for competition? Does it, for example, relate to historic information, or is it about future plans?), whether the information is available to all or only a select number of sellers, whether it forms a barrier to entry or expansion, and how detailed the information is (is it general statistical information, or specific information?).

In the US, the Supreme Court noted in *United States v United States Gypsum Co* that:

> The exchange of price data and other information among competitors does not invariably have anti-competitive effects; indeed, such practices can in certain circumstances increase economic efficiency and render markets more, rather than less, competitive. For this reason, we have held that such exchanges of information do not constitute a per se violation of the Sherman Act.

Note that the rule of reason may apply to exchange of price information. In *Todd v Exxon Corp.*, the Court of Appeals clarified that 'hardcore' price fixing is *per-se* unlawful and that information exchange may form a facilitating practice that can help support a price-fixing agreement. This should be distinguished from instances where 'the violation lies in the information exchange itself—as opposed to merely using the information exchange as evidence upon which to infer a price-fixing agreement. This exchange of information is not illegal per-se, but can be found unlawful under a rule of reason analysis.'

The DOJ and FTC have issued guidelines on 'Collaborations Among Competitors' in which they note that likely competitive harm may arise from the sharing of current or future information relating to price, cost, output, customers, or strategic planning. By contrast, the guidelines note that historic information or general information which is not company-specific will generally not raise competitive concerns. In a statement issued by the agencies with reference to the healthcare industry, they note that exchange of information is unlikely to give rise to competitive harm when the information is managed by a third party, when it concerns a number of market players, or when it is aggregated and reflects past activity.

It is worth noting that in addition to the application of Section 1 of the Sherman Act, Section 5 of the FTC Act prohibits 'unfair methods of competition' and may be applicable to harmful exchanges of information. Illustrative is the case of *Bosley, Inc.*, in which the FTC condemned the exchange of competitively sensitive, non-public information regarding business practices, future product offerings, price floors, and discounts between two competitors.

In Europe the analysis of information exchanges largely resembles that in the US. In its 'Guidelines on Horizontal Co-operation Agreements', the EU Commission discusses the assessment of information exchange under Article 101 TFEU. It notes that 'by artificially increasing transparency in the market, the exchange of strategic information can facilitate coordination (that is to say, alignment) of companies' competitive behaviour and result in restrictive effects on competition.' Information exchange may facilitate a collusive outcome when it eliminates uncertainties or increases transparency, thus dampening competition. It may further eliminate or undermine new entry to the market or exclude existing competitors from the market.

In *Fiatagri UK Ltd and New Holland Ford Ltd v Commission.*, the EU General Court considered information exchange arrangements between competitors. It noted that while in a competitive market information exchange may lead to the intensification of competition between suppliers, that will not be the case when the market is highly concentrated and information is exchanged frequently and in detail.

The EU Court and Commission distinguish between exchange of information which will be subjected to effects-based analysis and exchange of detailed price information which will be subjected to a presumption of illegality (object analysis). In its Guidelines on Horizontal Co-operation Agreements, the Commission notes that secretive information exchanges between competitors, which include individualized data regarding intended future prices or quantities, will be considered a restriction of competition by object. In *Dole Food Company*, the European Court of Justice considered pricing communications between competitors and held that: 'An exchange of information which is capable of removing uncertainty between participants as regards the timing, extent and details of the modifications to be adopted by the undertakings concerned in their conduct on the market must be regarded as pursuing an anti-competitive object.'

The court concluded that pricing communications had the objective of restricting competition. The approach taken here readily condemns specific price exchanges as object violations and removes them from the effects-based analysis. Note, however, that in principle it is open for the parties to show, even in an 'object' case, that the exchange of price information is exempted under Article 101(3) TFEU. While less likely to succeed, such an argument would involve proving that the exchange of price information improves production or distribution, allows consumers a fair share of the benefit, is indispensable to the attainment of these objectives, and does not eliminate competition in respect of a substantial part of the products in question.

Vertical agreements

Vertical agreements are those made between companies operating at different levels of the production or distribution chain. They govern the relationship between an upstream operator and a downstream distributor or retailer. For example, an agreement between a producer of food and a supermarket, or an agreement between a car manufacturer and a distributor of cars.

Vertical relationships generate fundamentally different market outcomes than horizontal collaborations. One striking feature, in this context, is the different incentives which affect the price setting function in the market.

Imagine a horizontal setting with two competing companies that sell a similar product. Both companies have an interest in market prices going up as this will increase their profitability. Competition law is there to curtail possible attempts to increase the price through anti-competitive agreements or collusion.

Now imagine a vertical agreement with one producer (upstream) selling its product at $10 to a distributor (downstream). What price would the producer likely wish the product to be sold at by the distributor? A high price, such as $60, or a lower price such as $20? The answer, in most cases, would be a lower price. Why? Because when the distributor charges its customers a lower price for the product, they buy more units. As they buy more units, the distributor purchases more units from the producers. Lower prices at the downstream level mean greater profits upstream for the producer. The producer has an interest to sell as many units as possible and, for this, it would not want the distributor to make an excessive profit. This is known as the 'self-policing' of vertical agreements, as the producer is likely to put pressure on the distributor to lower the selling price of the product.

Now, you may ask, but what if the producer sells a luxury product and does not want it to be sold too cheaply? What if the luxury image of the product merits the higher sum of $60? Well, if that were the case, the producer would have sold the product at a higher price to the distributor to get its fair share of the value. But the principle remains, once the product is sold, the producer does not benefit from any inflated sale price imposed by the distributor. In fact, often the producer will set a maximum or recommended price to protect its own interests.

Our example of 'self-policing' highlights the different incentives at stake, and why competition authorities are less concerned about vertical relations than horizontal agreements. The vertical relationship will often generate incentives which are in line with the consumer interest.

At times, however, restrictions in vertical agreements could raise concerns. While some restrictions may facilitate efficiencies, investment, and access to new markets, others may go too far and undermine competition. This may be the case, for example, when restrictions make it harder for competitors to enter the market (the 'foreclosure effect'), or when the vertical agreement significantly reduces competition at the level of production, distribution, or retail. In such instances a close examination of the agreement is called for in order to assess whether it has an anti-competitive effect.

We'll illustrate how possible anti-competitive effects are analysed using an example of an exclusive distribution agreement.

Exclusive distribution agreements

Imagine you manufacture a product and are looking for a distributor that will sell your product in a given territory. To ensure that the distributor promotes your product, you agree to the distributor investing in local advertisement and marketing and the pre- and post-sales service for your product. The dealer is willing to undertake this investment to become your distributor, but there is one problem: a 'free-rider' may undermine the agreement. The new distributor is concerned that if it invests in promoting your product, others may free-ride on its investment, taking advantage of the benefit without sharing the cost. While the distributor will need to charge a premium for each unit it sells (to cover the costs of promotions and sale services), others may be able to sell the product for less, including to customers who only want to buy the product because of the investing distributor's advertising and additional services.

To address this free-riding problem and incentivize the distributor to invest in services and promotions, the manufacturer will need to introduce some restrictions and conditions to the agreement. For example, the vertical agreement may include a provision which states that the distributor has exclusivity over a given territory allocated to it.

In both the US and the EU, the restriction would be acceptable when it is proportionate and necessary, resolves free-rider problems, and ensures investment in valuable pre-sale services. After all, without such a restriction, a distributor will refrain from any investment and as a result the customer will suffer.

In the US, exclusive territory allocation in distribution agreements is assessed under the rule of reason doctrine. Under this doctrine, US jurisprudence determines that most exclusive distribution agreements do not infringe antitrust law unless the manufacturer uses its market power to exclude competitors from a necessary distribution channel. Since the agreement in question only limits competition between distributors of the same brand (known as 'intra-brand competition'), it poses little concern as long as other competing brands are available on the market (that is, as long as there is sufficient 'inter-brand competition'). Accordingly, absent sufficient evidence of monopolization, non-price territorial restrictions will likely have no adverse effect on competition.

In Europe, on the other hand, the desire to protect the EU single market (which EU competition law is tasked with promoting) has led to a more restrictive approach. EU jurisprudence distinguishes between restrictions on 'active' and 'passive' selling. Restrictions on active sales prevent a distributor from actively seeking to sell its products outside its allocated territory (for example, by opening an outlet in another distributor's territory). Such restrictions may be justifiable to prevent the free-riding problem, and accordingly will be assessed for their effect on competition. On the other hand, when an agreement also includes restrictions on passive sale—that is, a provision which prevents distributor X from accepting unsolicited orders from customers who are based in another territory allocated to distributor Y—it is treated as an agreement with the object of restricting competition. The EU Court of Justice held in the case of *Consten & Grundig v Commission* that absolute territorial protection had the object of restricting competition. As held by the court:

> an agreement between producer and distributor which might tend to restore the national divisions in trade between Member States might be such as to frustrate the most fundamental objections of the [Union]. The Treaty, whose preamble and content aim at abolishing the barriers between states, and which in several provisions gives evidence of a stern attitude with regard to their reappearance, could not allow undertakings to reconstruct such barriers.

Most-favoured-nation clauses

To illustrate the nuanced analysis of effects, let us look more closely at parity clauses in vertical agreements. These clauses, also known as most-favoured-nation clauses (MFN), are sometimes used by a distributor to oblige its supplier to offer its goods or services at a price or terms which are equal or better than those offered by the supplier elsewhere. A parity clause could be narrow in nature (imposing limits on the supplier's ability to sell directly to customers at a lower price than that offered through the distributor), or wide in scope (imposing limits on the supplier's ability to sell at lower prices through other distribution channels as well as directly).

Think, for example, of an online platform operating a price comparison website for hotel reservations and bookings. These websites offer a listing of all available hotel rooms, from known to less-known hotels. For the potential customer, the online platform offers a convenient interface in which one can compare prices, read reviews, and make bookings while benefiting from after-sales support and guarantees. For the hotels, the online platform offers demand enhancing features, which may include marketing, advertising, and enhanced visibility. This may be significant, in particular, for small or less-known hotels which would otherwise find it difficult to reach the final customer and compete against more established hotels. For its services, the online platform typically charges a fee from hotels for every room booked through the price comparison website.

So far, so good. Now, let's see how MFN clauses may play a role in this relationship.

To ensure deals on the price comparison website are attractive to users, the platform may ask the hotels to agree not to sell their room at lower prices, or better terms, elsewhere—either on their own website (narrow MFN) or on other price comparison websites (wide MFN). Such a parity condition prevents the hotels from free-riding on the marketing efforts of the online platform—using it for free marketing, but then undercutting its price and completing the sale through alternative channels.

Should such restrictions in vertical agreements be allowed, or should they be considered anti-competitive?

The answer is not always simple. On the one hand, MFN clauses limit competition, could create price uniformity, and prevent suppliers from possibly offering better deals to consumers. On the other hand, these restrictions may be necessary to prevent free-riding and ensure platforms have the incentive to invest in demand and efficiency enhancing features.

The mixed benefits and drawbacks of MFN clauses call for a nuanced effect-based analysis which may result in different conclusions based on the scope of the restriction, the market characteristics, and the services offered by the platform.

By and large, wide MFN clauses have been condemned as anti-competitive. This is because they result in price coordination or alignment throughout the whole market and may soften competition between different platforms regarding the charges they levy on their suppliers.

By contrast, narrow MFN clauses (which only concern the relationship between a single platform and a single supplier, and do not govern the relationship between that supplier and other platforms) may offer a more acceptable balance between the desire to facilitate investment by the platform and the risk of potential anti-competitive effects.

In Europe, for example, a case which addressed the use of MFN clauses concerned Booking.com and its use of wide parity clauses in its dealing with hotels. Following an investigation by several European member states, Booking.com agreed to abandon the use of wide MFN clauses and replace them with a narrow restriction that limited the ability of hotels to offer lower prices on their own website, but enabled them to offer discounts offline, offer discounts to members of their loyalty clubs, and sell at lower prices on other platforms. These narrow restrictions were considered objectively necessary to ensure a fair and balanced relationship between Booking.com and hotel operators.

In the field of insurance, an interesting example, this time from the US, concerns action taken by the US DOJ against the insurer Blue Cross Blue Shield of Michigan, which had used wide MFN restrictions in its agreements with health providers. The parity provision required hospitals to charge the insurer a fee which is no more than what they charge its competitors. The DOJ found that the parity provision stifled competition and resulted in higher health insurance prices for Michigan consumers. Following legislation by the State of Michigan, which prohibited health insurers from using parity clauses in contracts with healthcare providers, the DOJ dismissed its antitrust lawsuit.

One last example, which triggered interest on both sides of the Atlantic, concerns the use of wide MFN clauses by Amazon. The issue was the subject of investigations in Europe, by the UK and German authorities as well as the European Commission. The agencies raised concerns regarding the impact of wide MFN clauses on suppliers' freedom to offer products at lower prices through competing platforms. Amazon addressed these concerns by agreeing to remove the parity clauses from its agreements with suppliers, and to stop enforcing them. The issue rose to the spotlight again, this time in the US, in a Congress report on 'Competition in Digital Markets' (released in 2020). The report noted that while parity clauses are not inherently anti-competitive, Amazon has made use of MFN clauses and its 'Fair Pricing Policy' to limit the ability of its suppliers or third-party sellers to 'collaborate with an existing or potential competitor to make lower-priced or innovative product offerings available to consumers'. The report raised concerns on the ability of rivals and new entrants to effectively compete against Amazon in the book distribution marketplace when such provisions are in place.

Two key takeaways emerge from our discussion of MFNs:

First, we can now better appreciate the nuanced analysis required of the pro- and anti-competitive effects of some restrictions. The analysis calls for consideration of a multitude of effects in market context, evaluation of the incentives to invest and compete, possible efficiencies, and possible adverse impact on consumers and sellers.

Second, we learned that sometimes a 'lowest price guarantee' offered by a platform, or seller, reflects nothing more than a contractual arrangement which restricts others from undercutting the price and making you a better offer. As they say, all that glitters is not gold.

Chapter 9
Monopolies and the abuse of market power

In many instances, bigger is better. Bigger companies usually benefit from economies of scale, efficiencies, and power, all of which enables them to offer better services at lower prices and promote valuable innovation, to our benefit.

Look, for example, at our online environment and our use of social networks. Most of us use the leading provider. You likely appreciate the fact that many of your friends use it as well, the fact that it can offer many related services, that it has the resources to ensure reliability and that it offers innovation when possible. Being 'big' enables your social network to benefit from 'economies of scale' (cost advantages and efficiencies made possible by the increased volume of operation). It also improves its 'network effects' as you and your friends benefit from a wider set of potential contacts as the network expands (this is known as 'direct network effects'). The increase in number of users also makes the network more attractive to advertisers and sellers (this is known as 'indirect network effects').

When a company grows 'big' by offering a better product or service, it may also increase its market power. We appreciate its service and, as a result, more of us will purchase from this company rather than its competitors. That company is winning the competition and gaining market power. Since this is a natural outcome of the competitive process, being 'big' as a result of legitimate competition is not condemned by the competition and antitrust laws.

Accordingly, competition enforcers are mindful that a company that becomes powerful by being better than others and winning the process of competition should not be penalized for its efforts. If it were, this would likely chill its incentive to compete. As noted by the US Supreme Court in *Verizon Communications Inc. v Law Offices of Curtis V. Trinko*:

> The mere possession of monopoly power, and the concomitant charging of monopoly prices, is not only not unlawful; it is an important element of the free-market system. The opportunity to charge monopoly prices—at least for a short period—is what attracts 'business acumen' in the first place; it induces risk taking that produces innovation and economic growth. To safeguard the incentive to innovate, the possession of monopoly power will not be found unlawful unless it is accompanied by an element of anti-competitive conduct.

While big is not necessarily bad, 'big' companies that benefit from distinct market power are subjected to further responsibilities. The law prevents these large, powerful companies from distorting competition and abusing their powers. Laws dealing with market power, and its possible misuse, aim to strike a delicate balance—refraining from chilling competition and innovation (by accepting that market power may be the result of a legitimate competitive process, a superior product, or business acumen), while preventing powerful companies from distorting competition by abusing their market position. In line with this, the law does not seek to limit the ability of the powerful company to compete, nor does it seek to protect smaller competitors from legitimate competition unleashed by it.

Market power

The first step in applying competition law to misuse of market power is the identification of such power. This, as illustrated above, is a pre-condition for the application of the law. If you have no market power—if you are a small or medium-size company that operates in a competitive market setting—you will not be subjected to these provisions.

So how powerful should you be to be deemed to have market power that could trigger antitrust intervention (in the case of misuse of power)?

The answer to this question may differ in each jurisdiction. Many jurisdictions will use the benchmark of 'dominant position', some will use 'monopoly power' or 'monopolization', while others may focus on the presence of a 'superior bargaining position'. The use of different terminology in the law may naturally affect the application of a relevant law in each jurisdiction and the conclusions therein. A company may be regarded to have market power in one jurisdiction, but not in another. For our discussion, we can simplify our review, and focus on the common attributes that are used to establish market power in all jurisdictions.

The starting point of the analysis lies in the definition of the relevant market (discussed in Chapter 2). Once the boundaries of the market are set, one can draw conclusions as to the relative size of the company in question. Remember that when considering market power, we do not ask how 'big' the company is in sizable terms, but how powerful it is in the context of a given market. Accordingly, a large company may have limited market power if the market is wide, while a small company might have a significant market share and power when operating on a very narrow market.

This is why, many times, companies accused of an abuse of market power or monopolization will start their defence by challenging the market definition. If they are successful in arguing that the defined market should be wider, they may be able to show that the wider market includes many more products or competitors. As a result, the relative size of the company in question becomes smaller and it would exercise less market power. Let us illustrate this: think of the pizza example mentioned earlier in this book. Imagine that you are a lawyer or an economist and your client produces and sells frozen pizzas. Your client is accused of abusing its market power on the market for frozen pizza in territory X. In that market there are three companies, one of them being your client which occupies 80 per cent of that market. To challenge that accusation, your first line of defence may be to focus on the market definition, arguing that the market was wrongly defined and that it is wider than the market for frozen pizza in territory X. You might argue that the market includes all frozen foods, or all frozen ready meals, or all chilled and frozen pizzas. You might argue that the territory in question goes well beyond X. If the product and/or the geographical market are deemed to be wider, then the relative size of your client will drop significantly. In such a case, the issue of market power is muted.

Your second line of defence will likely focus on the question of power. After the market has been defined, you may try to show that, even if your client appears 'big' in relative terms, it does not necessarily benefit from market power. To examine market power, we must shift our focus to the market characteristics and the ability of the company to exercise power on that given market. A range of indicators will be considered to evaluate the presence of market power. Among them:

- The market share of the company in question: it is generally accepted, in the absence of evidence to the contrary, that a very large market share (typically, above 50 per cent) supports the conclusion that a company benefits from market power.

- The market shares of other companies operating on that market. Are other competitors powerful enough to be able to restrict the operation of the company in question? If they are, then customers may join them if the company charges them higher prices or offers lower quality goods.

- The presence of barriers to entry which reduce the threat of potential competition.

- Market characteristics such as market dynamism, innovation levels, concentration levels, the presence of distribution networks, network effects, and other elements which affect the competitive process.

- The legal and regulatory environment and relevant intellectual property rights that could hinder or encourage competition.

These indicators, among others, are used to reach a conclusion as to the ability of a company to exercise market power. Companies accused of having market power will often challenge that conclusion and claim that, despite the market characteristics, they cannot price profitably above competitive price levels. They will often seek to show that it is impossible for them to operate independently of consumers and other rivals, and as a result they lack the ability to engage in exclusionary or exploitative practices.

The illicit use of market power

Having reviewed the analysis of market power, let us now consider which actions may amount to illicit use of market power. This is where things get a little bit complicated as there are a range of views as to which actions should be condemned and which actions are acceptable. While competition agencies around the world often agree about the dividing line between pro-competitive and anti-competitive activity, they do occasionally disagree. In the application of competition law and cartel agreements, all jurisdictions adopt a common approach worldwide. Yet, the application of the law regarding monopolies and market power continues to differ in various jurisdictions.

Such differences may arise from the language of the law, as some jurisdictions use narrow categories of illicit conduct while others capture a wider range of activities. For example, in some jurisdictions excessive pricing may be condemned as abusive action, while others accept it as part of the competitive process.

Differences may also arise due to varying views as to the ability of the market to self-correct, and the approach to error costs arising from over- or under-intervention. These differences may affect the nature of cases being pursued by different jurisdictions, and the prioritization of cases, as well as the standard of proof required by the law in order to prove a violation. The higher the standard, the more evidence one needs to establish a violation. By requiring very high proof of effects, it may become impossible to establish a violation, allowing dominant companies to escape scrutiny. On the other hand, a low standard may require little evidence, resulting in over-prosecuting companies even where harm is neither present nor likely to occur.

Let us illustrate this heterogeneity by looking at the US and EU approaches.

In the US, Section 2 of the Sherman Act condemns any monopolization, attempt to monopolize, or conspiracy to monopolize trade or commerce. The Section targets illicit behaviour by firms which have or are close to attaining market power. In recent decades the law has been interpreted strictly and applied in a limited manner to ensure that enforcement does not chill the competitive process. As put eloquently by Judge Learned Hand in *United States v Aluminum Company of America*: 'The successful competitor, having been urged to compete, must not be turned upon when he wins.' This approach led to an ongoing narrowing of the principles of harm used to establish monopolization, and similarly led to a decrease of enforcement actions at the federal level. The risk of over-enforcement (that is, the fear that enforcement action will condemn pro-competitive and efficient actions), coupled with the assumption that market forces often resolve competitive concerns, has fuelled this narrowing trend. Demonstrating this trend, in the first two decades of the 21st century, the US DOJ brought only one standalone monopolization case under Section 2 of the Sherman Act.

Some have argued that the scope of Section 2 of the Sherman Antitrust Act has been heavily restricted over the years, which as a result has enabled powerful companies to operate freely even when consumer harm is present. The range of potential illicit activities is relatively narrow, and the standard of proof required to prove a violation is too high. With the rise of digital markets and increased public debate on the need for intervention, there have been clear signs that the US DOJ and FTC have now taken a more interventionist approach, as they challenge some of the actions taken by leading digital platforms.

Across the Atlantic, in the EU, Article 102 TFEU condemns the abuse of a dominant position. Large companies with power in a given market have a special responsibility not to distort competition on the market and are prohibited from abusing their market position. By contrast to the US, the EU provision has been more widely applied—both in terms of legal scope and authorities' propensity to bring enforcement actions. Abuse of dominance cases represented roughly 23 per cent of the 138 competition enforcement actions in Europe in the single year of 2019, reflecting European authorities' greater willingness to constrain unilateral anti-competitive conduct.

EU law has been interpreted to capture a wider range of illicit conducts than US provisions. Most notable is the application of Article 102 TFEU to behaviours of exploitation, including the charge of excessive pricing. Other examples include the wider use of the EU provision in cases of refusal to supply, refusal to license, and margin squeeze.

The differences in enforcement action, standard of proof, and categories of abuse have naturally led to some inconsistencies in enforcement. Whereas the EU has considered some actions by dominant firms with market power to amount to an abuse, the US has, at times, considered similar actions to be legitimate, or has applied different thresholds to establish illegality.

We'll illustrate the differences by looking at several categories of abuse and monopolization, and explore one case study.

Predatory pricing

This practice involves charging prices below cost, as part of a strategy to exclude a competitor. A company with market power that benefits from deep pockets may use this strategy to push other competitors out of the market. The company will sell its product below cost, at a loss, making it harder for competitors to remain on the market. Once the competitors are pushed out of the market, the company will increase the price, and benefit from greater market domination. Consumers who may have welcomed the short-term price reduction will face much higher prices once competitors are eliminated. Both the EU and the US condemn predation, but they differ in their threshold for intervention.

In *Brooke Group Ltd v Brown & Williamson Tobacco Corp.*, the US Supreme Court considered the charge of predatory pricing alongside the other elements of a monopoly claim. The court held that the plaintiff must prove (1) that the defendant set its prices so low that they are below 'an appropriate measure of its...costs'; and (2) that there is a 'dangerous probability' that the defendant will recoup the losses it incurs through low pricing by driving out rivals, thereby enabling it to charge monopoly prices.

In practice, it has been difficult for plaintiffs in the US to meet *Brooke Group*'s requirements. The courts have adopted a rigid notion of recoupment (that is, the requirement to show that following the predatory phase, the increase in prices will be high enough to subsidize the predatory strategy). Access to data on the monopolist's costs structure challenges the ability to establish below-cost pricing and recoupment.

By contrast, EU competition law has set a lower threshold for illegality, making it easier to establish predatory pricing. In *Akzo*, the General Court accepted that predation can be established even when a dominant company prices above average variable costs, as long as its intent to eliminate a competitor has been proven. In *Tetra Pak*, the Court of Justice confirmed that EU law does not require proof of recoupment in order to establish predation.

As one would expect, the different threshold for illegality will result in varying conclusions in each of the jurisdictions.

Excessive pricing

In Europe, Article 102 TFEU makes clear reference to direct or indirect imposition of unfair purchase or selling prices. In *United Brands*, the court stated that excessive pricing by a dominant undertaking may be abusive under Article 102 TFEU, and that prices are excessive when they have no reasonable relation to the economic value of the product supplied.

The enforcement against excessive pricing has been relatively limited across Europe, and used mostly in cases where market failure or barriers to entry prevent the market from self-correcting. The difficulty in identifying what would have been the competitive price, and in determining whether current levels of price are excessive enough to merit intervention, led the European Commission and other enforcers to exercise caution in finding this abuse for fear of becoming 'price regulators'. Still, the ability to intervene when the market dynamic fails is seen as an important deterrent, and reflects the overall aim of EU competition law, which is to ensure fairness in the relationship between dominant sellers and their customers.

By contrast to the position in the EU, Section 2 of the Sherman Act is not used to penalize exploitative activities, such as the charging of high prices by powerful companies. The US Supreme Court has upheld this position in several instances, stating that the US antitrust law does not prohibit lawfully obtained monopolies from charging monopoly prices. In *Trinko*, the court held that the ability to charge high prices 'is an important element of the free-market system' that underpins the competitive process. This policy is based on the assumption that the possibility of charging high prices as a monopolist is the reward which incentivizes firms to compete, invest, and excel. At the same time, market forces ensure that such high prices will attract new market entry, leading the market to correct itself. And, so, the mere threat of entry will often lead monopolies to refrain from pricing excessively over a prolonged period.

Refusal to supply or license

US and EU antitrust authorities also differ in their approach to cases involving a dominant company's refusal to supply goods or to license key technology to its competitors. US antitrust rules generally hold that a dominant company has no obligation to supply or to license to its competitors, and refusal to deal with one's competitors is not an antitrust harm. The US Supreme Court reaffirmed this general principle most recently in 2004 in *Verizon v Trinko*, noting that Section 2 of the Sherman Act 'does not restrict the long recognized right of [a] trader or manufacturer engaged in an entirely private business, freely to exercise his own independent discretion as to parties with whom he will deal.'

In US law, there do remain a few exceptions to this general principle. The most prominent involves a dominant company's decision to terminate a long-standing and mutually profitable commercial relationship without a good commercial justification (other than to hurt its competitor). This principle was confirmed in 1985 by the US Supreme Court in *Aspen Skiing v Aspen Highlands Skiing*. Aspen Skiing terminated an agreement with its weaker competitor Aspen Highlands, which allowed customers to purchase a pass to access both companies' ski lifts. Customers then shunned Aspen Highlands in favour of Aspen Skiing's much larger network of ski lifts. The Supreme Court found that Aspen Skiing's termination was anti-competitive because it terminated an existing, long-standing, and mutually profitable business opportunity, for which there was substantial consumer demand.

US commentators generally struggle to reconcile *Aspen Skiing* and other exceptions with the general principle that a company has no obligation to deal with its competitors, and restrictions on refusals to deal play a very minimal role in US antitrust. Recognizing this minimal role, the US DOJ notes in its enforcement guidance that:

> The Department believes that there is a significant risk of long-run harm to consumers from antitrust intervention against unilateral, unconditional refusals to deal with rivals, particularly considering the effects of economy-wide disincentives and remedial difficulties. The Department thus concludes that antitrust liability for unilateral, unconditional refusals to deal with rivals should not play a meaningful part in Section 2 enforcement.

In contrast to this restrictive approach adopted in the US, Europe has taken a more interventionist stance. In a number of cases, dominant companies were held to abuse their position when they refused to grant access, to supply, or to license technology to another company operating downstream. Key here is the use of power by the dominant company over an input, and it leveraging this power to improve its own operation in a downstream market. The EU courts have been clear that while a dominant company has the right to refuse to supply or license another company, such refusal may, in exceptional circumstances, amount to an abuse of a dominant position. This may be the case when the refusal to supply concerns a product which is indispensable for carrying on the business in question, prevents the appearance of a new or improved product, and is likely to exclude all effective competition in the secondary market.

The *Google Shopping* case

Our discussion so far illustrates some of the variations in enforcement scope and attitude on both sides of the Atlantic. Reflecting on our earlier discussion on the adequate level of intervention, you would be right to wonder whether the EU over-intervenes or the US under-intervenes. Which ideology promotes better, more competitive markets? Which promotes efficiency? Not surprisingly, the answers to these questions may vary widely depending on whom you ask. Like many things in antitrust, there isn't necessarily an easy answer to these questions (and those who offer one might simply disguise ideology as facts).

To demonstrate the difference in approach and the complexity of analysis, let's focus on one case which triggered different interventions in Europe and the US—the case of *Google Shopping*.

We all benefit from the digital revolution and from waves of innovation, efficiency, and consumer welfare. Indeed, the digital economy has transformed the way we communicate, engage, and consume. It heralded an era of perceived opulence, where more is the norm, and where our needs are anticipated and catered for. One of the pivotal engines of that revolution has been our ability to search for goods, services, and information online.

Online search engines provide a road map for the user. They ensure information flows and improve the efficiency of online markets for goods, services, and ideas. A key player and innovator in this field has been Google, which offers us an effortless search engine. So successful is the engine, that Google has attained a position of market power in many states. If you are looking for something online, you simply 'Google' it. This has turned Google into a key entry point into the market. After all, if your business does not appear on Google search, we may not know about it.

And here is where things get interesting. In 2017, following years of investigation, the European Commission fined Google €2.42 billion for abusing its dominant position in the market for general internet search by giving an illegal advantage to its own comparison shopping service, thereby stifling competition in the downstream market for comparison shopping. The Commission found that Google benefited from market power in the market for internet search and leveraged this power to another downstream market for shopping services. By doing so, Google was able to beat the competition on that downstream market, despite its own product (on that downstream market) being inferior to competing products.

In its decision, the Commission asserted that Google's own comparison shopping service had not been gaining traffic and was ranked low on Google's own general search results pages. To improve traffic to its own shopping site and divert it from other shopping sites, Google had systematically given prominent placement to its own comparison shopping service, always placing it at the top of any search results, and had not subjected the service to Google's generic search ranking algorithms. Other rival comparison shopping services, which were subject to Google's generic search algorithms, faced new rules that pushed sites which display third-party content (a feature inherent to comparison shopping services) down in the ranking. The result—users would see the Google shopping service at the top of their search results and would have to look further to find competing services on subsequent pages.

In its decision, the Commission did not object to the criteria used to design Google's generic search algorithms. Nor did the Commission object to a rule which demotes the ranking of sites which display third-party content. The objection was to Google not subjecting its own shopping service to the same conditions as competing services. This self-favouritism, the Commission argued, amounted to an abuse of Google's dominant position.

In its analysis, the Commission considered data on how Google's practices shaped user behaviour. It concluded that the change in ranking adversely impacted traffic to other comparison shopping services. While the competitor may be a click away, competition isn't. That is, consumers lack incentive and awareness to change online service providers and are easily captured by the key platforms, to the detriment of other competing services and users. This affected other providers' revenues and income from merchants or online search advertising. The Commission concluded that Google's conduct foreclosed the market and pushed out competing comparison shopping services.

In addition to fining Google, the Commission required Google to give equal treatment to rival comparison shopping websites, and to apply the same methods and processes when positioning its own and competing services.

Google challenged the decision in court and argued that the practice did not amount to abusive favouritism. It claimed that its practices were aimed at improving quality, rather than driving traffic to a Google comparison shopping service. As of February 2021, the appeal is pending and awaiting the judgment of the European General Court.

Across the Atlantic, the US FTC also investigated claims that Google's practice distorted competition downstream. The FTC considered the allegations that Google unfairly gave preference to its own content on the Google search results page and selectively demoted its competitors' content from those results. The FTC concluded that the changes introduced by Google had legitimate business justifications and were mainly driven by the desire to improve the quality of its search product and the overall user experience. The negative impact on competitors downstream, being demoted in the search results, was incidental to the otherwise legitimate goal to improve the interface so as to quickly answer and better satisfy its users' search queries:

> We ... recognize that some of Google's algorithm and design changes resulted in the demotion of websites that could, collectively, be considered threats to Google's search business ... These changes resulted in significant traffic loss to the demoted comparison shopping properties, arguably weakening those websites ... On the other hand, these changes to Google's search algorithm could reasonably be viewed as improving the overall quality of Google's search results because the first search page now presented the user with a greater diversity of websites. Product design is an important dimension of competition and condemning legitimate product improvements risks harming consumers.

The FTC noted that competing general search engines also introduced similar design changes, suggesting that these were quality improvements with no necessary connection to anti-competitive exclusion. Following its assessment of the case, in 2013, the FTC reached a unanimous decision to close the investigation.

The clear indication from the FTC that there was no evidence of illicit conduct was later put in doubt when an internal FTC report was leaked to the press. The leaked report outlined concerns raised by some FTC staff who favoured filing a suit against Google.

Others, including the FTC economic staff, were of the opposite opinion. While possible disagreement within any agency is not unique, the leaked document underscores the complexity at hand and the difficulty of separating efficiency enhancing measures from exclusionary tactics. The EU Commission's investigation and imposition of a fine in 2017 led to renewed calls in the US to reopen the investigation into Google's practices, as well as to investigate other allegations. These calls were largely rejected at the time.

The Google shopping case demonstrates the complexity and possible heterogeneity in approach to these competition questions on either side of the Atlantic. By contrast to the investigation of cartel agreements, it may be difficult to draw the line between illicit abusive behaviour and pro-competitive actions. Differences in ideology, economic modelling, and base assumptions may result in diverging outcomes.

Ongoing evolution

Moving beyond the specific facts of the *Google Shopping* case, it is worth noting that, as markets evolve, so does the approach towards intervention. This trend has been most noticeable with respect to digital markets. The evolution of digital markets has seen the rise of big data, big analytics, extreme network effects, and increased concentration. Network effects notably facilitated the rise of key platforms, gatekeepers, and the creation of new ecosystems. Network effects also cause some markets to 'tip' towards dominant incumbents, causing runaway growth at the expense of their competitors.

These changes have triggered greater scrutiny around the world. Several competition agencies and international organizations have closely monitored the changing market dynamics, and recommend greater scrutiny as markets become more concentrated. Several reports and hearings, in the EU, the US, and elsewhere, have acknowledged the rising power of internet giants and the possible need for greater intervention. They have noted that digital markets subjected to tipping effects may result in entrenched and dominant companies which are able to exploit consumers and exclude competitors.

In line with these developments, one may identify a distinct change in attitude towards monopolization in digital markets in the US.

In 2019, the FTC, DOJ, and attorney generals of many states have started looking at a range of possible infringements by dominant internet giants. The year 2019 also saw the initiation by the House Judiciary Committee of a bipartisan investigation into the state of competition online.

A year later, in 2020, the signs of change became more apparent. Congress released its report on the state of competition online, and raised significant concerns about the power of platforms, their anti-competitive strategies, and the distortion of competition and innovation. The report identified a pressing need for legislative action and reform.

Antitrust enforcement has also intensified. Of note is the civil antitrust lawsuit filed by the US DOJ, along with eleven state attorney generals, to stop Google from unlawfully maintaining monopolies through anti-competitive and exclusionary practices. The complaint opened with direct acknowledgement of the changing digital market reality:

> Two decades ago, Google became the darling of Silicon Valley as a scrappy startup with an innovative way to search the emerging internet. That Google is long gone. The Google of today is a monopoly gatekeeper for the internet, and one of the wealthiest companies on the planet, with a market value of $1 trillion and annual revenue exceeding $160 billion. For many years, Google has

used anticompetitive tactics to maintain and extend its monopolies in the markets for general search services, search advertising, and general search text advertising—the cornerstones of its empire.

The complaint alleges that Google suppressed competition and engaged in unlawful foreclosure that had harmful effects on consumers, competition, and innovation. The DOJ asked the court to instruct Google to bring these anti-competitive practices to an end and consider the possible need for structural relief (restructuring of the company) to cure any anti-competitive harm.

The rapid evolution of markets and change in enforcement attitude offer us an opportunity to critically reflect on the timing and effectiveness of antitrust enforcement and the adequate level of intervention. Was the FTC correct when it closed the Google investigation in 2013? Is current intervention sufficient, or is it too late to restore competition online? Or, rather, do current enforcement actions reflect over-intervention which risks chilling competition, investment, and innovation?

Chapter 10
Mergers and acquisitions

When a company wants to expand its business, obtain new technology, or reach new markets it may seek to acquire or merge with another company. Such transactions may offer economies of scale, efficiencies, synergies, and innovation.

Take, for example, two regional airlines. Each operates its own reservation system, maintenance framework, and logistics. Each has to negotiate deals with suppliers and the airports it uses. Being of small or medium size may affect the airline's ability to generate efficiencies in operation, to secure preferable rates from airports, and to procure airplanes at an attractive price. A merger between these two airlines may help obtain these efficiencies and economies of scale. It may help them negotiate better deals with airports and other suppliers. It may open up better finance deals which create opportunities for investment and expansion. These efficiencies can deliver lower prices to customers, who will also benefit from greater choice of travel routes offered by the new merged entity.

So where is the problem?

While of potential benefit to society, mergers, takeovers, share acquisitions, and joint ventures also affect the market structure, and at times may reduce competition. When markets become more concentrated following a merger, we move further away from a competitive market structure to a structure in which market power might undermine the competitive process.

To address this risk, the competition agency must assess the impact of the transaction—consider the efficiencies and other benefits stemming from the combination of power and possible adverse effect due to a lessening of competitive pressure on the market.

Here we'll explore the appraisal of mergers and acquisitions in more detail.

Notifying a merger transaction

To ensure they can intervene to stop a merger, most competition agencies operate a pre-emptive regime in which merging parties notify transactions before putting them in motion. This type of pre-emptive analysis that looks at a proposed transaction prior to its occurrence is known as *ex-ante* appraisal (and differs from the *ex-post* analysis discussed in previous chapters that dealt with anti-competitive agreements or monopolization).

With over 120 jurisdictions operating variations of merger control regimes worldwide, parties to large international mergers are often required to notify a number of competition regimes and undergo a parallel assessment before they receive outright or conditional approval of their transaction.

Each jurisdiction designs its own merger regime. In most jurisdictions, merging parties must notify the jurisdiction if their domestic and worldwide turnover exceeds certain thresholds. The thresholds are used as proxy for likely effect. If the merging entity has significant economic activity within a jurisdiction (above the threshold set in law) the competition agency will want to know about it ahead of it being implemented.

In the EU, for example, Regulation (EC) 139/2004 on 'The Control of Concentrations between Undertakings' (EU Merger Regulation) sets the thresholds for notification. The Regulation will apply to transactions that have a significant worldwide and Community-wide turnover. Merging entities which satisfy these criteria must notify their transaction to the European Commission prior to its implementation. The parties must then suspend the transaction until the Commission reaches a decision. The first phase of the investigation may last around four weeks, at the end of which a transaction may be approved, approved with conditions, or referred to a second phase. The second phase may last around 13 weeks and at the end the transaction may be approved, approved with conditions, or blocked by the European Commission.

In the US, the Hart-Scott-Rodino Antitrust Improvements Act of 1976 sets the thresholds for notification. Notification is required when parties to a sizable transaction engage in commerce and have significant assets or annual net sales. Such large transactions need to be notified to the FTC and the Justice Department. Once the parties notify the transaction, they enter an initial waiting period of 15 to 30 days. At the end of that period they may proceed with the transaction, unless the competition agency raises competitive concerns, extends the waiting period, or requires the companies to provide further information. Following an investigation, the agency may seek an injunction in court to prevent the transaction.

The substantive assessment

Once notified, the competition agency will assess the proposed transaction by considering its possible pro-competitive and anti-competitive effects. The analysis is predictive, as the agency has to consider whether the combination of two or more companies will affect the market structure in a way that is likely to lead to a significant decrease in competition.

In Europe, Article 2(2) of the Merger Regulation sets out the substantive test against which transactions are assessed: it focuses on whether the transaction would 'significantly impede effective competition' in the internal market, particularly as a result of the creation or strengthening of a dominant position (this is often referred to as 'the SIEC test'). In the US, Section 7 of the Clayton Act outlines the benchmark for assessment, and prohibits mergers and acquisitions that 'substantially lessen the competition' or tend to create a monopoly (this is often referred to as 'the SLC test').

While the wording of the SIEC and SLC tests differs, they provide a similar analytical framework. Indeed, the essence of the analysis is similar in both the EU and the US, as well as elsewhere around the world.

By and large, competition agencies begin the appraisal process by defining the relevant product and geographical markets. This helps the agency to understand the boundaries of competition and the relationship between the parties to the transaction.

Having defined the market, the agency will consider how the market reality will likely change if the merger proceeds. Variables include: the market shares of the parties and their competitors before and after the transaction; levels of market concentration; possible barriers to entry and expansion; the effects on actual and potential competition; effects on suppliers and buyers; the presence of powerful suppliers and buyers; possible effects on investment and innovation; relevant contractual arrangements; and regulatory regimes. With this information, the agency can assess the post-merger reality, including the likelihood of price increases or other changes adverse to customers.

Transactions may raise different competitive concerns depending on the parties' market relations. The analysis of proposed transactions would therefore differ based on whether they are horizontal, vertical, or conglomerate.

Horizontal transactions

Horizontal transactions involve competitors operating on the same level of production or distribution. A horizontal merger reduces the number of companies present in the relevant market, leading to an increase in concentration and a reduction in competition. These transactions may give rise to concerns when they result in 'unilateral' or 'coordinated' effects.

'Unilateral effects' (also known as non-coordinated effects) stem from the elimination of competition between the merging parties. These effects are often of concern when the new merged entity benefits from greater market power. Following the increase in market power and its improved bargaining position, the merged entity may have the ability and incentive to unilaterally increase the price of some of its products above the pre-merger level. Eliminating competition between the merging parties may also reduce the merged entity's product variety or innovation efforts.

'Coordinated effects' arise when a merger between two firms changes the way in which other firms behave in the market. Here the change in market structure following the transaction may give rise to explicit or tacit coordination between the firms. Parallel accommodating conduct or interdependence of action among market participants may result in higher prices and dampening of competition, as explored in Chapter 6.

Vertical transactions

Vertical mergers involve companies that operate at different levels in the chain of production and distribution—for example, a transaction which combines a producer and distributor of a given product. A transaction which combines vertically related entities may deliver distinct efficiencies in distribution. Furthermore, it eliminates double marginalization (creating one profit unit rather than two) and subsequently can reduce prices for downstream buyers. At times, however, vertical transactions can raise concerns.

They may result in 'unilateral effects' when the merged entity has the ability and incentive to foreclose the competitive opportunities of other market participants by limiting their access to inputs or customers. The vertically integrated company may weaken or exclude competitors by raising their costs, preventing them from accessing its distribution network or using sensitive information about rivals (that it gained from the transaction).

A vertical merger may result, at times, in 'coordinated effects' when the change in market structure, following the transaction, diminishes competition by enabling or encouraging coordination. When the conditions for tacit collusion are present, the interdependence of action would dampen competition as companies refrain from undercutting other companies' prices.

Conglomerate transactions

Conglomerate transactions take place between companies that have neither horizontal nor vertical relationships and are active in separate markets. These transactions rarely raise anti-competitive concerns. However, when the parties to the transaction operate in separate yet closely related markets, the transaction may, in limited circumstances, trigger intervention:

'Unilateral effects' may materialize when the transaction leads to foreclosure of other companies. The merged entity may, for example, benefit from a significant degree of market power that enables it to exclude competitors from the market. Anti-competitive effects may arise from conditioning of sales and other exclusionary strategies which enable the merged entity to push 'just as efficient' competitors out of the market.

'Coordinated effects' may arise when the transaction facilitates market transparency and interdependence which results in tacit coordination.

Remedies and commitments

Competition agencies clear most merger transactions which come before them, allowing the parties to proceed with the transactions. When, however, a transaction gives rise to competition concerns, the parties and the competition agencies generally discuss possible commitments and remedies which can resolve these concerns.

In most cases, remedies involve a structural change to the transaction that addresses the competition agency's concerns about a transaction. A structural remedy can involve divesting part of the corporate group of its assets, which is aimed at restoring competition. The sale may create a new independent entity on the market, strengthen an existing competitor, or facilitate new entry to the market.

In some cases, agencies may deem an access remedy appropriate to resolve the competitive concerns. Access remedies may, for example, include the licensing of key technologies to a new entrant or existing competitor, or the provision of access to key infrastructure or networks.

In some particular circumstances a behavioural remedy may address some competitive concerns. The merged entity will commit to behave in a certain way to eliminate future concerns. These remedies are infrequently used, as competition concerns in merger control often arise from adverse changes to the market structure. Because of this, behavioural remedies will rarely offer a good solution that can eliminate the concerns.

All in all, remedies enable the parties to go ahead with a modified transaction, after they have addressed the competition agency's concerns. As such, they play a major role in shaping the market following a transaction. They introduce versatility and fine-tuning which allows some of the benefits associated with mergers and acquisitions while safeguarding the competitiveness of the market.

Procedure

There are important procedural differences between the European administrative system—in which the Commission appraises the case, reaches a decision, imposes remedies, and may block a transaction—and the US system. In the US, the procedure differs depending on whether the FTC or DOJ challenges the transaction, but by and large it requires the competition agencies to present their case in court if they oppose the transaction.

This is an important distinction. In Europe, the administrative nature of the process empowers the Commission to reach a decision with no intervention from the court. The EU General Court will only hear a case if it is appealed (by parties applying to annul the Commission's decision). On appeal, the court will not consider all the facts from the start (*de novo*), but rather it will consider whether the Commission has made an error in its analysis. EU case law states that it is not for the General Court to substitute its own assessment for that of the Commission.

The *Bayer/Monsanto* transaction

To illustrate the complexity involved in merger appraisal, as well as the parallel application of US and EU merger regimes, let us look at the transaction between Bayer and Monsanto.

Bayer, a large German producer of pharmaceutical and chemical products (including crop chemicals), made a bid to purchase Monsanto, a leading American producer of seeds and developer of crop protection products. The proposed $66 billion mega-transaction was to result in Bayer owning and controlling Monsanto's business. It would enable Bayer to widen its primary focus on healthcare to include the agrochemical business. The new company was to act as a supplier that catered to all of the farmers' needs—seeds, seed traits, biologicals, pesticides, and digital farming technology. The acquisition was expected to eliminate double mark-ups, create distinct efficiencies, and promote innovation, saving billions in costs.

Against these efficiencies stood the fact that the takeover would create a giant company operating in an already heavily consolidated agrochemical industry (following earlier 'mega-deals' which included the state-owned ChemChina acquiring Swiss Syngenta, and Dow Chemical merging with DuPont). The industry was further characterized by high barriers to entry and expansion, due to very high research and development costs, the centrality of intellectual property rights and patents, and the need for regulatory know-how. In this already concentrated market, Bayer would turn into the world's biggest supplier of pesticides and seeds for farmers, with distinct advantages, including in digital farming and data markets.

Being of such mammoth scale and significance, the deal required approval from a large number of regulators around the world, among them the EU Commission and the US DOJ.

The European Commission concluded its investigation in March 2018 (9 months after the first formal notification). During the course of its investigation, the Commission assessed more than 2,000 different product markets and reviewed millions of internal documents. It identified the merged entity as the 'leading global integrated player with respect to seeds and traits, herbicides and insecticides' and 'the number two player regarding fungicides... across geographic regions'. The Commission noted that the new company would be 60 per cent larger than the next two largest global 'integrated players', ChemChina and DowDuPont.

Due to the degree of complementarity between the Bayer and Monsanto businesses, the Commission raised concerns that the transaction would lead to reduced horizontal competition. It found that the acquisition would strengthen or create a dominant position in several markets, including seed traits, crop protection, and digital agriculture.

The Commission was particularly concerned with the effects the transaction would have on innovation efforts and investment. It was argued that the combination of the two companies would adversely affect their existing research and development efforts. Due to the overlaps between the innovation pipelines of each company, the transaction risked dampening competition on innovation.

To address the horizontal concerns, and allow the transaction to be cleared, Bayer agreed to sell more than $7 billion worth of assets to BASF (the fourth largest industry player with a substantial crop protection business). The sales include Bayer's vegetable seeds and certain other seeds and traits businesses, seed treatment and pesticide businesses (notably those in competition against Monsanto's Roundup herbicide). Bayer also agreed to license part of its research and all of its digital agriculture business to BASF.

The commitments prevented the elimination of competitive pressure, by putting BASF in a position to constrain Monsanto in the same way that Bayer would have done before the acquisition.

In the US, the DOJ reviewed the transaction and raised concerns regarding the effects that horizontal and vertical integration might have on American farmers and consumers. The US investigation focused on the market for genetically modified (GM) seeds and traits, which is of central importance in the US but largely prohibited in Europe. Bayer and Monsanto were close competitors in the GM seed market for cotton, canola, and soybeans. The transaction would have eliminated the fierce competition between them and increased their power in these markets. In addition, the DOJ raised concerns as to the combination of power in the market for herbicides (the elimination of competition between Monsanto's Roundup and Bayer's Liberty products). In the market for seed treatment, the DOJ pointed to both horizontal effects and the risk of vertical foreclosure.

In April 2018, the DOJ and the parties reached an agreement in principle to clear the transaction subject to commitments. To address the DOJ's concerns, Bayer agreed to divest $9 billion of businesses and assets, and sell them to BASF. The commitments in the US broadly aligned with the EU Commission by using BASF to replace Bayer as an independent and vigorous competitor in each of the affected markets.

Thus, the challenging transaction was cleared, with conditions, in both the EU and the US, enabling the companies to proceed with the combination of their businesses. The remedies enabled the competition agencies to ensure markets remained competitive, while allowing the companies (and ultimately customers) to benefit from the synergies and efficiencies that came with the businesses' integration.

The competition tale of the *Bayer/Monsanto* transaction may have reached a satisfying conclusion following its approval. But the story continues as the joint entity had little time to celebrate and benefit from the hoped-for synergies and efficiencies. When buying Monsanto and its assets, Bayer also bought risk and legal liability.

Prior to the transaction, a large number of suits were filed against Monsanto, claiming that its glyphosate-based Roundup herbicide caused non-Hodgkin lymphoma. Bayer was aware of these claims, but had failed to fully appreciate the severity and scale of the allegations and the momentous liability they carried. By the time the acquisition was complete, internal Monsanto documents came to light, revealing the company was aware of the health concerns and the risks associated with the use of Roundup. What followed were a string of judgments against Bayer (which had by then acquired Monsanto, and was now responsible for its past actions and liabilities). The once celebrated mega-deal led to mega-compensation payments, and a sharp drop in Bayer's share price. At some point, Bayer's market capitalization had fallen to the point where the value of Monsanto had 'almost entirely evaporated'. This extraordinary turn of events demolished the value that the transaction had aimed to achieve and tarnished Bayer's brand. The company has since recovered, but the tale serves as a reminder of the risks and uncertainties involved in merger transactions as well as the difficulty in predicting the evolution of markets.

Chapter 11
The international dimension

Recent decades have witnessed a marked increase in international trade and cross-border activities. Our global environment is characterized by imports and exports, multinational corporations and international supply chains. Companies in foreign jurisdictions sell products and services to customers in others. And as trade goes global, so do the potential restrictions on competition.

In the field of competition law an infringement can have consequences within a given territory even though the conduct that caused those consequences occurred and may even have been completed elsewhere. In order to protect their domestic markets, competition agencies often need to apply their national laws beyond the boundaries of their state. At times, a single activity by a company may be condemned and fined by several jurisdictions which were affected by it. Sometimes, one jurisdiction may object to an activity that has been cleared by the local jurisdiction in which it took place, but nevertheless affects competition within the first-mentioned state. Indeed, some of the cases mentioned earlier in this book involved the application of EU and US laws to companies that are formally incorporated and based in one jurisdiction, but have business activity in others.

This type of cross-border enforcement is known as 'extraterritorial' application of the law. This long-arm jurisdiction is the reason why managers and directors in one country will think twice before entering into a collusive cartel agreement that sells products into other jurisdictions. It is the reason that directors residing in one jurisdiction may be extradited and tried in another, and that companies may be penalized by foreign agencies for cartel activities (for example, the *Air Cargo Cartel* case; Chapter 7). It is also the reason that a company based in one territory may be fined and penalized by another territory for anti-competitive activities such as abuse of dominance (for example, the *Google Shopping* case; Chapter 9). It is why companies that wish to merge may have to notify the transaction to other jurisdictions and be subject to their merger review (for example, the *Bayer/Monsanto* transaction; Chapter 10).

Extraterritoriality in competition law commonly relies on one of two legal concepts. The first extends a competition regime's jurisdiction to activities which have an effect on that regime's markets. The second is more restricted in nature and requires 'implementation' of anti-competitive activity within the given territory as a condition for extraterritorial application of domestic laws.

In the US, the effects doctrine enabled the enforcement of antitrust laws on foreign companies. In the EU, both the effects and implementation doctrines may be used to apply the competition provisions to foreign companies.

Extraterritorial application of US antitrust law

The Permanent Court of International Justice in The Hague (the forerunner to today's International Court of Justice) initially recognized states' ability to apply their law extraterritorially based on 'effects' in the *Lotus* case in 1927, which addressed the extent of states' criminal jurisdiction over acts causing a collision in open sea. In subsequent years, the US used this doctrine to establish the long-arm jurisdiction of its antitrust law. In *United States v*

Aluminum Company of America, the US Second Circuit Court asserted that 'any State may impose liabilities, even upon persons not within its allegiance, for conduct outside its borders, which has consequences within its borders, which [the] State reprehends; and these liabilities other States will ordinarily recognize.' In subsequent cases, including *Timberlane Lumber Co. v Bank of America* and *Metro Industries Inc v Sammi Corp*, the courts applied the effects doctrine in a more restrictive way, requiring not only a direct and substantial effect within the US, but also that the US's interests should be weighed against the interests of other states involved. Other cases followed a more expansive approach as laid down by the Supreme Court in *Hartford Fire Insurance Co. v California.*

Although different in their tone and emphasis, the cases from the US courts share the notion that, under certain conditions, finding a direct and substantial effect within US territory enables the assertion of US jurisdiction. The extraterritoriality of US antitrust law protects the US market against cartels and illicit activities carried out by companies outside the US that adversely affect American customers. The law's extraterritorial application strengthens cartel enforcement and enables the US to prosecute companies and individuals based outside US borders, as long as their actions adversely affect competition within the US.

Extraterritorial application of EU competition law

In Europe, the extraterritorial application of competition law evolved differently. In the early days of enforcement, the European Court of Justice took a narrower approach, and refrained from clearly and directly adopting the effects doctrine. In its rulings, the Court of Justice preferred to limit itself to the well-recognized territoriality principle, which established jurisdictions over acts within the borders of a state. For example, in the *Wood Pulp* judgment, the Court of Justice held that jurisdiction under EU law exists over firms outside the Union if they implement a price-fixing agreement reached outside the EU by selling to purchasers within it.

As EU competition law developed, the EU General Court introduced the effects doctrine into EU case law to augment the territoriality principle. In *Gencor Limited v Commission*, the General Court considered the application of the EU Merger Regulation to transactions between foreign companies. It acknowledged the implementation principle established in *Wood Pulp*, but went on to decide that the transaction was subject to the European Merger Regulation on the basis of its immediate, foreseeable, and substantial effects in the Union.

In *Intel Corporation v Commission*, the General Court clarified the legal position and held that EU competition laws apply extraterritorially when the activity was either implemented in the EU or when it led to a substantial, direct, and foreseeable effect on EU markets. The two benchmarks are not cumulative but rather offer alternative approaches for the purposes of establishing extraterritorial jurisdiction.

International cooperation and harmonization

The extraterritorial application of competition and antitrust laws provides a valuable instrument to protect the local market. However, this unilateral approach comes with a cost of possible friction. After all, if several agencies apply their own national laws to the same transaction or activity, we may end up with inconsistent decisions and remedies. This 'system friction' may result in an activity being deemed legal in one jurisdiction and condemned in another. It may result in one competition agency requiring merging parties to divest part of their activities to address a competitive concern, and another requiring them to divest a different part of their business.

To minimize the potential friction resulting from extraterritoriality, while allowing jurisdictions to protect their local markets, agencies and states engage in international cooperation at bilateral and multinational levels.

Bilateral agreements

Bilateral agreements establish close collaboration between two jurisdictions in their enforcement efforts. While each jurisdiction maintains its sovereignty, it assists and shares information with the other and may take into account the other's interests.

Take for example the EU/US Competition Cooperation Agreement. Signed in 1991, the agreement provides the basis for long-standing collaboration between the jurisdictions. It provides for the agencies to notify each other of their cases, allows the exchange of information on competition enforcement, and facilitates cooperation and coordination between the agencies. The cooperation agreement ensures that each party will take account of the other party's interests when it enforces its competition rules. Over the years, the close cooperation between the agencies has led to marked assimilation and coordination of action in the EU and the US.

This cooperation is evident in merger analysis; the agencies routinely notify each other of ongoing investigations, exchange views on the relevant markets and the impact the transaction may generate, and coordinate remedies when appropriate. The close cooperation between the agencies has also led to remarkable convergence of thought and analysis, and greater consistency and legal certainty for the companies involved. As part of their mutual efforts to facilitate coordination, the agencies issued best practice guidelines on cooperation in merger review which adopt similar analytical approaches. In the guidelines they note that their ongoing cooperation has been 'beneficial not only for the agencies, but also for merging parties and third parties, as it increases the efficiency of the respective investigations, reduces the burden on merging parties and third parties, and increases the overall transparency of the merger review process.'

Regional and multinational cooperation

As more competition problems transcend national boundaries, there has been an emphasis on supplementing the select number of bilateral agreements with wider membership initiatives. Regional and multinational cooperation initiatives facilitate harmonization of enforcement approaches among many agencies.

The success of these efforts has varied over the years, depending on the scope of membership and the nature of the agreements. Wide membership agreements may be difficult to implement due to the complexity of the multinational arena and the domestically oriented nature of competition enforcement. One can distinguish between two types of wide membership initiatives—*binding* and *voluntary* frameworks.

Binding frameworks, as the name suggests, bind all those who sign them to follow the principles outlined in the agreement. Despite theoretically being an ideal instrument to advance collaboration, they are difficult to develop due to the differences in market and political conditions, and unwillingness of many jurisdictions to limit their sovereignty and independence of action. Several failed attempts of the international community to advance wide membership binding frameworks reflect this difficulty. Noteworthy are the failed attempts to include detailed competition provisions as part of the Havana Charter, World Trade Organization (WTO), or other wide membership binding initiatives for an international competition code, such as one proposed by the Munich Group of experts.

Voluntary frameworks provide for 'soft law' initiatives which create a focal point for competition agencies with no binding effect. The agreed principles do not bind the members, but are used to advance a process of convergence and dialogue. These frameworks support assimilation and cooperation, and have brought wide consensus on policy, economics, and law. A number of organizations have supported this ongoing international dialogue and have been active in proliferating internationally agreed guidelines. Worthy of note is the International Competition Network (ICN), which provides competition authorities from all over the world with a specialized venue for maintaining regular contacts and addressing practical competition concerns. The ICN has successfully advocated for the adoption of internationally agreed standards and procedures in competition policy around the world. Alongside the Organisation for Co-operation and Development (OECD) and the United Nations Conference on Trade and Development (UNCTAD) it serves as one of the leading venues which facilitate capacity-building and wide-membership international cooperation.

The limitations of cooperation

Overall, the proliferation of competition regimes worldwide provides powerful support to greater competitiveness of local and global markets. With increased cooperation and collaboration, the international landscape has displayed increased harmonization of thought and enforcement efforts.

It is, however, important to understand the limitations of international cooperation. With so many jurisdictions applying domestic competition provisions, some inconsistency is inevitable.

To begin with, cooperation links independent competition agencies that apply their national laws. When the laws differ in goals, scope, and application, we may witness different decisions on similar matters, despite close collaboration. Similarly, the

Competition and Antitrust Law

enforcement capacity of each jurisdiction, and its enforcement agenda and priorities, may differ. An enforcement action which is deemed attractive and helpful in one jurisdiction may be regarded as the wrong cure in another.

Second, as each jurisdiction considers the factual matrix and economic theory, it may give different weight to some arguments over others. Differences in interpretation of facts and application of economic models may result in inconsistent outcomes. Communication between agencies may limit inconsistency in application, but it will not necessarily eliminate it.

Third, at times the market reality differs between jurisdictions. Even when dealing with the same activity or transaction, if the market is local or regional, the effects will differ and so will the outcome. For example: a merger transaction between two dairy product manufacturers that operate globally may have varying effects in different regional markets for these products, as local regulation, consumption habits, and market characteristics differ.

Still, despite these possible inconsistencies and the limitations of cooperation, it is important to remember and stress that the core competition enforcement tale remains similar worldwide. More often than not, we witness consistency in application of the principles, in the theories of harm, and in the remedies used. While the drive towards competition homogeneity does not override the domestic reality, national law, and the autonomy of agencies, it has brought us closer to a commonality of understanding and similarity of enforcement.

Final reflections

Free competitive markets can deliver an abundance of welfare to consumers. The goal of greater competition is common to all enforcement regimes and embedded in their DNA, even if the methods and languages may differ.

As our understanding of markets and economic theory evolves, so does the application of competition law. The letter of the law may have remained unchanged, but implementation never stagnates. Looking back at our enforcement policies, we can see instances of over- and under-intervention. With the wisdom of hindsight, we can try to improve our current policies and make sure that we engage in optimal enforcement.

One cannot escape the normative dimension of competition policy. Your view on the role that markets and competition play in society and their relations to other values will affect the application of the law and the evolution of economic theory. Behind the objective façade are values that may change and, as they do, so does the application of competition law. With changing market and socio-political realities, the enforcement challenges become apparent.

Digital markets

Consider, for example, the rise of digital markets, briefly mentioned in Chapters 8 and 9, and the effect this has on the enforcement of competition and antitrust laws. On the one hand, the digital economy offers us a clear path to future prosperity, delivering waves of innovation, efficiency, and consumer welfare. It has transformed the way we communicate, engage, and consume, and heralded an era of perceived opulence, where more is the norm and where our needs are anticipated and catered for. On the other hand, our digital economy has seen the rise of big data, big analytics, extreme network effects, and increased concentration. Key gatekeepers have emerged, and increasingly control our online interfaces and our access to goods and services. We have seen pricing practices which are driven by artificial intelligence and automated algorithms that may be used to reduce competition. We have also seen the increased use of personalized pricing as our data is harvested and analysed to support discriminatory practices. Online platforms may control whole ecosystems and determine the dynamics of competition. They control what you see, the news you read, and, ultimately, the market for ideas. Alongside the many benefits of technology, one can easily see the risks. How should competition law enforcement react to these developments? Should we intervene, or should we assume that markets will self-correct?

These questions require us to consider afresh the scope of competition law, our treatment of data and network effects, the effectiveness of competition enforcement, and the possible need for pre-emptive or regulatory measures. They require us to check our assumptions as to market dynamics, the likelihood of disruptive innovation, and the level at which market power may be achieved. They require us to move beyond traditional economic theory, and consider human behaviour and biases as we seek to establish the true presence of outside options and competitive pressure.

Planet in crisis

Now let us turn to a very different challenge in our environment. At the time of writing, the COVID-19 pandemic has shaken societies and economies across the globe. Manufacturing and long supply chains have been heavily disrupted, and retail has shrunk to unprecedented levels. Some markets failed to deliver. The ideal global market vision, with its economies of scale and scope, was disrupted and challenged as countries realized its limitations.

At the same time, with mounting pressure to develop and produce a vaccine, scientists and pharmaceutical companies engaged in collaboration. Competing supermarket chains, coping with limited supply, also needed to coordinate their action, stock management, and deliveries. Competition enforcement had to adapt to this new reality. Indeed, many competition agencies released special temporary guidelines to facilitate urgent cooperation in the short term and allow businesses to cope with unprecedented economic disruption. Actions which would otherwise have triggered antitrust intervention were deemed permissible for the greater good. At the same time, several jurisdictions had to increase scrutiny to stop consumers being exploited or subjected to excessive pricing.

This extraordinary challenge, the change to market dynamics, and the change to enforcement priorities raises interesting questions as to the role of competition enforcement in modern society. Having relaxed our enforcement approach to address the pandemic, should we do the same to address wider concerns? Which societal goals should triumph? Is competition more important to us than our other values? Should it be treated as one of many tools used to deliver future prosperity or as a stand-alone goal?

With a view to our planet, the threat to our environment may necessitate cooperation among competitors which in normal times may infringe competition laws. Should we apply the same determination when looking more broadly at climate change and sustainability issues? And if so, where should we draw the dividing line between pro-competitiveness and anti-competitiveness?

So, what is the right formulation of competition policy?

Our competition ideology is affected by the political landscape and the affinity of the government with trade and big businesses. It is affected by our societal values and our views about fairness and the distribution of wealth in society. It is affected by our economy being developed or developing; by our attitude towards nationalism or globalization. It is affected by the changing market realities and the dynamics of competition. It is affected by our beliefs as to the self-correcting capacity of markets and whether this delivers optimal results. It is affected by our understanding of economic theory, the base assumptions we rely on, and our desire for legal and business certainty. It is affected by our legal systems, their flexibility, and the rule of law. It is affected by our view of the relationship between government and free markets. And it is affected by public debate, the media, consumer groups, businesses, lobbyists, and money.

Indeed, if one observes how competition law enforcement has developed over the past century, an evolving journey emerges. At different stages of economic development and political circumstances, different jurisdictions have used competition enforcement to advance varied goals.

Between clearly anti-competitive practices (such as price-fixing cartels) and pro-competitive rivalry, lies a vast continuum which brings out the complexity in competition law enforcement and its susceptibility to national variations, culture, policies, and politics. A grey area which reminds us of the lack of clear absolute benchmarks for illegality. Unsurprisingly, that area makes us all feel uncomfortable. After all, it would be much tidier to advance an enforcement policy with mathematical certainty, but that is simply not possible. Complex economic and legal analysis applied to complex market dynamics cannot always deliver a binary result.

One's personal notion of the right recipe for a prosperous society is a reflection of this complex landscape, rather than a manifestation of an absolute truth. Those who claim to have the true recipe for competition enforcement, a pure recipe that overrides any other opposing argument, do little more than dress their own ideology in cloaks of superior objectivity. These claims may be naïve or promote a given agenda. Either way, they offer a distorted image of the complex nature of competition policy. The key to effective competition law enforcement lies not in the pretence of purity or certainty, but in an open and informed debate on the law and economics, and a vision of the society to which we aspire.

Remember this: competition policy both reflects and affects society. It affects the money in your pocket, the goods and services you buy, and the innovation from which you benefit. It affects the distribution of wealth and the level of inequality around you. It affects the powers that govern your behaviour, corporate culture, and much more. It affects your life, your autonomy, your privacy. It could affect the market for ideas, plurality, and—ultimately—democracy.

Such a policy that affects the very fabric of society certainly merits our close attention.

Further reading

There are several textbooks that offer a more detailed introduction to competition law, antitrust law, competition policy, and market economics. Among them are:

D Bailey and LE Johnson, *Bellamy & Child: European Union Law of Competition* (OUP, 8th ed, 2019)

D Broder, *US Antitrust Law and Enforcement: A Practice Introduction* (OUP, 3rd ed, 2016)

E Elhauge and D Geradin, *Global Competition Law and Economics* (Hart Publishing, 2nd ed, 2011)

J Faull and A Nikpay, *The EU Law of Competition* (OUP, 3rd ed, 2014)

DJ Gerber, *Competition Law and Antitrust* (OUP, 2020)

W Kovacic and J Wright, *Antitrust Law in Perspective: Cases, Concepts and Problems in Competition Policy* (West Academic Press, 3rd ed (rev), 2017)

S Marco Colino, *Competition Law of the EU and UK* (OUP, 8th ed, 2019)

G Niels, H Jenkins, and J Kavanagh, *Economics for Competition Lawyers* (OUP, 2nd ed, 2016)

R Whish and D Bailey, *Competition Law* (OUP, 9th ed, 2018)

Several monographs and collections offer a critical review of the enforcement of competition and antitrust laws and the role of competition in society. Among them are:

G Amato, *Antitrust and the Bounds of Power: The Dilemma of Liberal Democracy in the History of the Market* (Hart, 1997)

A Ayal, *Fairness in Antitrust: Protecting the Strong from the Weak* (Hart, 2016)

JB Baker, *The Antitrust Paradigm: Restoring a Competitive Economy* (Harvard, 2019)

RH Bork, *The Antitrust Paradox* (Simon & Schuster, 1978)

DW Carlton and JM Perloff, *Modern Industrial Organization* (Pearson, 4th ed, 2004)

TK Cheng, *Competition Law in Developing Countries* (OUP, 2020)

A Ezrachi and ME Stucke, *Virtual Competition: The Promise and Perils of the Algorithm-Driven Economy* (Harvard, 2016)

E Fox and D Crane, *Antitrust Stories* (Foundation Press, 2007)

C Fumagalli, M Motta, and C Calcagno, *Exclusionary Practices: The Economics of Monopolisation and Abuse of Dominance* (CUP, 2018)

MS Gal, *Competition Policy for Small Market Economies* (HUP, 2003)

D Gerard and I Lianos, *Reconciling Efficiency and Equity: A Global Challenge for Competition Policy* (CUP, 2019)

H Hovenkamp, *The Antitrust Enterprise* (HUP, 2005)

K Hylton, *Antitrust Law: Economic Theory & Common Law Evolution* (CUP, 2010)

J Nowag, *Environmental Integration in Competition and Free-Movement Laws* (OUP, 2017)

R Pitofsky, *How the Chicago School Overshot the Mark: The Effect of Conservative Economic Analysis on U.S. Antitrust* (OUP, 2008)

RA Posner, *Antitrust Law* (Chicago Press, 2nd ed, 2001)

ME Stucke and A Ezrachi, *Competition Overdose: How Free Market Mythology Transformed Us from Citizen Kings to Market Servants* (Harper Business, 2020)

W Wils, *Principles of European Antitrust Enforcement* (Hart, 2005)

References

Chapter 1: The power of competition

A Smith, *The Wealth of Nations* (first published 1776, Penguin Classics, 1982)

Brooke Group Ltd v Brown & Williamson Tobacco Corp., 509 U.S. 209 (1993)

William WHITE et al., v R.M. PACKER CO., INC., et al., 635 F.3d 571, 579 (1st Cir. 2011)

Chapter 2: Markets

M Vestager, 'Defining markets in a new age' Chillin' Competition Conference, Brussels (9 December 2019) <https://ec.europa.eu/commission/commissioners/2019–2024/vestager/announcements/defining-markets-new-age_en> accessed 31 July 2020

Commission Notice on the definition of relevant market for the purposes of Community competition law (97/C 372/03)

United Brands v Commission (27/76), [1978] ECR 207, [1978] 1 CMLR 429

FTC v Whole Foods Market (23 April 2008, No. 07–5276)

US v E.I. duPont De Nemours & Co. 351 U.S. 377 (1956)

In the Matter of DaVita, Inc., Docket No. C-4152

Chapter 3: The goals and scope of competition and antitrust laws

A Ezrachi, 'Sponge' *J of Antitrust Enforcement* 5 (2017): 49

J Kirkwood and R Lande, 'The fundamental goal of antitrust: protecting consumers not increasing efficiency' *Notre Dame LRev* 84 (2008): 191

The Sherman Antitrust Act of 1890

The Treaty establishing the European Economic Community ('the Rome Treaty') 1957

Treaty on the Functioning of the European Union (TFEU) 2012/C 326/01

Consolidated version of the Treaty on European Union (TEU) 2012/C 326/01

Commission (EC), XXIInd. Report on Competition Policy 1992, 13

Anti Monopoly Law, Article 1 (China)

Act on the Prohibition of Private Monopolization and Maintenance of Fair Trade (Act No. 54 of 14 April 1947) ('The Antimonopoly Act' (Japan)), Article 1

Monopoly Regulation and Fair Trade Act (MRFT) Article 1

Fair Trade Act 2011 (Taiwan), Article 1

Competition Act 2003 (No. 2 of 2003) (Namibia)

The Competition Act, 2012 (India), Section 54

The Competition Ordinance (Cap 619) (Hong Kong), Sections 9, 24

Enterprise Act 2002 (UK), chapter 2

Decision by Lord Mandelson, the Secretary of State for Business, not to refer to the Competition Commission the merger between Lloyds TSB Group plc and HBOS plc under Section 45 of the Enterprise Act 2002 (31 October 2008). A challenge to the legality of the decision was subsequently dismissed by the Competition Appeal Tribunal: 1107/4/10/08 *Merger Action Group v Secretary of State for Business, Enterprise and Regulatory Reform* [2008] CAT 36 (10 December 2008). Cf. competitive concerns identified by the OFT in *Anticipated acquisition by Lloyds TSB plc of HBOS plc: Report to the Secretary of State for Business, Enterprise and Regulatory Reform* (No. ME/3862/08, 24 October 2008), 27–58

S42 des deutschen Gesetzes gegen Wettbewerbsbeschränkungen (GWB)

Bundeskartellamt Press Release, 'Bundeskartellamt prohitis E.ON/ Gelsenberg (Ruhrgas) merger' (21 January 2002) <http:// www.bundeskartellamt.de/SharedDocs/Meldung/EN/ Pressemitteilungen/2002/21_01_2002_EON_eng.html> accessed 31 July 2020

Chapter 4: What is the optimal level of enforcement?

ME Stucke, 'Reconsidering antitrust's goals' *Boston College Law Review* 53 (2012): 551, 609

S Bishop, 'Snake-oil with mathematics is still snake-oil: why recent trends in the application of so-called "sophisticated" economics is hindering good competition policy enforcement' *Eur Competition J* 9 (2013): 67

WE Kovacic, 'The influence of economics on antitrust law' *Economic Inquiry* 30 (1992): 294

European Commission, *Google Search (Shopping)* (AT.39740) (27 June 2017)

Federal Trade Commission, *In the Matter of Google Inc.* (FTC File Number 111–0163) (3 January 2013)

European Commission, 'Competition policy for the digital era' DG COMP (20 May 2019)

Federal Trade Commission, 'Big data: a tool for inclusion or exclusion? Understanding the issues' (January 2016)

Report of the Digital Competition Expert Panel (UK), 'Unlocking digital competition' ('The Furman Report') (March 2019)

Australian Competition & Consumer Commission, 'Digital platforms inquiry: final report' (June 2019)

Autorité de la Concurrence, 'Contribution de l'Autorité de la concurrence au débat sur la politique de concurrence et les enjeux numériques' (19 February 2020)

Bericht der Kommission Wettbewerbsrecht 4.0, 'Ein neuer Wettbewerbsrahmen für die Digitalwirtschaft' (9 September 2019)

UNCTAD Intergovernmental Group of Experts on Competition Law and Policy, 'Competition issues in the digital economy' (1 May 2019)

OECD (2018) 'Rethinking antitrust tools for multi-sided platforms'

Chapter 5: The legal framework

The Sherman Antitrust Act of 1890

Board of Trade of Chicago v US, 246 U.S. 231 (1918)

Leegin Creative Leather Products, Inc. v PSKS, Inc 551 U.S. 877 (2007)
  Agnew v National Collegiate Athletic Association, 683 F.3d 328, 347 (7th Cir. 2012)

US v E.I. duPont De Nemours & Co. 351 U.S. 377 (1956)

Spectrum Sports, Inc. v McQuillan, 506 U.S. 447, 456 (1993)

TFEU 2012/C 326/01, *Competition Authority v Beef Industry Development Society Ltd and Barry Brothers (Carrigmore) Meats Ltd* (Case C-209/07), [2008] ECR I-08637

Groupement des Cartes Bancaires (Case C-67/13 P), [2014] CMLR 22

Société Technique Minière (LTM) v Maschinenbau Ulm GmbH (MBU) (Case 56/65), [1966] ECR 235

Hoffmann-La Roche (Case C-179/16), [2018] 4 CMLR 13

Chapter 6: Who enforces the law?

The Sherman Antitrust Act of 1890

The Federal Trade Commission Act of 1914, Section 5

D Feinstein, FTC Bureau of Competition, 'A few words about Section 5' (13 March 2015) <https://www.ftc.gov/news-events/blogs/competition-matters/2015/03/few-words-about-section-5> accessed 31 July 2020

Council Regulation (EC) No. 1/2003 on the implementation of the rules on competition laid down in Articles 81 and 82 of the Treaty (16 December 2002), Article 9

Chapter 7: The fight against cartels

M Monti, 'Fighting cartels: why and how? Why should we be concerned with cartels and collusive behaviour?' (3rd Nordic Competition Policy Conference, Stockholm, 11–12 September 2000) <https://ec.europa.eu/commission/presscorner/detail/en/SPEECH_00_295> accessed 31 July 2020

V Ghosal and DD Sokol, 'The rise and (potential) fall of U.S. cartel enforcement (2020) *University of Illinois Law Review* 471

Office of General Counsel, US Sentencing Commission, 'Antitrust Primer' (February 2019) <https://www.ussc.gov/sites/default/files/pdf/training/primers/2019_Primer_Antitrust.pdf> accessed 31 July 2020

TFEU 2012/C 326/01, Article 101

The Sherman Antitrust Act of 1920, Section 1; as amended by the Criminal Antitrust Penalty Enhancement and Reform Act of 2004

US v Florida Cancer Specialists & Research Institute, LLC, No. 2:20-cr-78 (M.D. Fla. April 30, 2020)

Council Regulation (EC) No. 1/2003 on the implementation of the rules on competition laid down in Articles 81 and 82 of the Treaty (16 December 2002), Article 23

European Commission, *Trucks* (Case AT.39824) (27 September 2017)

European Commission, *Forex* (Case AT.40135) (16 May 2019)

The Alternative Fines Act, 18 U.S.C. § 3571

Company Directors Disqualification Act 1986 s9A, as inserted by the Enterprise Act 2002

European Commission, *Airfreight* (Case AT.39258) (17 March 2017)

In re Air Cargo Shipping Services Antitrust Litigation, 278 F.R.D. 51 (E.D.N.Y. 2010)

Department of Justice (Press Release), 'Extradited former air cargo executive pleads guilty for participating in a worldwide price-fixing conspiracy' (23 January 2020) <https://www.justice.gov/opa/pr/extradited-former-air-cargo-executive-pleads-guilty-participating-worldwide-price-fixing> accessed 31 July 2020

European Commission (Press Release), 'Antitrust: Commission re-adopts decision and fines air cargo carriers €776 million for price-fixing cartel' (17 March 2017) <https://ec.europa.eu/commission/presscorner/detail/en/IP_17_661> accessed 31 July 2020

OECD Global Forum on Competition, 'Crisis cartels' (18 October 2011) <http://www.oecd.org/daf/competition/cartels/48948847.pdf>

Chapter 8: Horizontal and vertical agreements

A Ezrachi, 'The competitive effects of parity clauses on online commerce' *European Competition Journal* 11/2–3 (2015): 488–519

TFEU 2012/C 326/01, Article 101

US v US Gypsum Co., 438 U.S. 422 (1978)

Todd v Exxon Corp., 275 F.3d 191 (2d Cir. 2001)

Federal Trade Commission and the US Department of Justice, 'Antitrust guidelines for collaborations among competitors' (April 2000)

US Department of Justice and the Federal Trade Commission, 'Statements of antitrust enforcement policy in health care' (August 1996)

The Sherman Antitrust Act of 1890, Section 1

Federal Trade Commission Act of 1914, Section 5

Federal Trade Commission, *In the Matter of Bosley, Inc.* (FTC File No. 121 0184, Docket No. 1564624)

French Competition Authority, Decision No. 15-d-06 of 21 April 2015 on the practices implemented by Booking.com in the online hotel reservation sector

United States v. Blue Cross Blue Shield of Michigan, 809 F. Supp. 2d
    665 (E.D. Mich. 2011)

European Commission, 'Guidelines on the assessment of horizontal
    mergers under the Council Regulation on the control of
    concentrations between undertakings' (2004/C 31/03) OJ C 265
    (18 October 2008)

European Commission, 'Guidelines on the assessment of non-horizontal
    mergers under the Council Regulation on the control of
    concentrations between undertakings' (2008/C 265/07)
    OJ C 267 (22 October 2008)

US Department of Justice and the Federal Trade Commission,
    'Horizontal merger guidelines' (19 August 2010)

US Department of Justice and the Federal Trade Commission,
    'Vertical merger guidelines' (30 June 2020)

*Fiatagri UK Ltd and New Holland Ford Ltd v Commission (UK
    Agricultural Tractor Registration Exchange)* (Case T-34/92
    General Court), [1994] ECR II-905

Dole Food Company (C-286/13P), [2015] 4 CMLR 16

Consten S.a.R.L and Grundig-Verkaufs-GmbH v Commission (Joined
    Cases 56 and 58/64), [1966] ECR 299, [1966] CMLR 418

Subcommittee on Antitrust, Commercial and Administrative Law,
    'Investigation of competition in digital markets' (6 October 2020)
    <https://judiciary.house.gov/uploadedfiles/competition_in_
    digital_markets.pdf> accessed 21 October 2020

Chapter 9: Monopolies and the abuse of market power

P Areeda and DF Turner, 'Predatory pricing and related practices
    under Section 2 of the Sherman Act' *Harvard LRev* 88 (1975): 697

J Vickers, 'Market power in competition cases' *Eur Competition J* 2
    (2006): 3

Verizon Communications Inc v Law Offices of Curtis V. Trinko LLP
    (02–682), 540 US 398 (2003)

The Sherman Antitrust Act of 1890, Section 2

US v Aluminum Company of America (Alcoa) 148 F.2d 416
    (2 Cir. 1945)

The Thurman Arnold Project at Yale, 'Antitrust enforcement data'
    (*Yale School of Management*) <https://som.yale.edu/faculty-
    research-centers/centers-initiatives/thurman-arnold-project-at-
    yale/antitrust-enforcement-data-0> accessed 31 July 2020

TFEU 2012/C 326/01, Article 102

European Competition Network, 'Statistics' (*European Commission*)
    <https://ec.europa.eu/competition/ecn/statistics.html#2> accessed
    31 July 2020

Brooke Group Ltd v Brown & Williamson Tobacco Corp., 509 U.S. 209
    (1993)

AKZO Chemie BV v Commission (C-62/86), [1991] ECR I-3359,
    [1993] 5 CMLR 215

Tetra Pak International SA v Commission (C-333/94 P—Tetrapak II),
    [1996] ECR I-5951, [1997] 4 CMLR 662

United Brands v Commission (27/76), [1978] ECR 207, [1978] 1
    CMLR 429

Aspen Skiing Co. v Aspen Highlands Skiing Corp., 472 U.S. 585,
    605 (1985)

Department of Justice, 'Competition and monopoly: single-firm
    conduct under Section 2 of the Sherman Act' (September 2008)

European Commission, *Google Search (Shopping)* (AT.39740)
    (27 June 2017)

Federal Trade Commission, *In the Matter of Google Inc.* (FTC File
    Number 111-0163) (3 January 2013)

US Department of Justice (Press Release), 'Justice Department
    reviewing the practices of market-leading online platforms'
    (23 July 2019) <https://www.justice.gov/opa/pr/justice-
    department-reviewing-practices-market-leading-online-
    platforms> accessed 31 July 2020

Subcommittee on Antitrust, Commercial and Administrative Law,
    'Investigation of competition in digital markets' (6 October 2020)
    <https://judiciary.house.gov/uploadedfiles/competition_in_
    digital_markets.pdf> accessed 21 October 2020

US Department of Justice v Google (20 October 2020) Case
    1:20-cv-03010

Chapter 10: Mergers and acquisitions

Regulation (EC) 139/2004 on 'The control of concentrations between
    undertakings' (EU Merger Regulation)

The Hart-Scott-Rodino Antitrust Improvements Act 1976

The Clayton Act 1914

US Department of Justice and the Federal Trade Commission,
    'Horizontal merger guidelines' (19 August 2010)

US Department of Justice and the Federal Trade Commission,
    'Vertical merger guidelines' (30 June 2020)

European Commission, 'Guidelines on the assessment of horizontal mergers under the Council Regulation on the control of concentrations between undertakings' (2004/C 31/03) OJ C 265 (18 October 2008)

European Commission, 'Guidelines on the assessment of non-horizontal mergers under the Council Regulation on the control of concentrations between undertakings' (2008/C 265/07) OJ C 267 (22 October 2008)

European Commission, *Bayer/Monsanto* (Case M.8084) (21 March 2018)

European Commission (Press Release), 'Mergers: commission clear Bayer's acquisition of Monsanto, subject to conditions' (21 March 2018) <https://ec.europa.eu/commission/presscorner/detail/en/IP_18_2282> accessed 31 July 2020

US v Bayer AG et al, No. 1:18-cv-01241, Document 25 (D.D.C. 2019); see also the DOJ's Competitive Impact Statement, Document 3 (D.D.C. 2018)

US Department of Justice (Press Release), 'Justice Department secures largest negotiated merger divestiture ever to preserve competition threatened by Bayer's acquisition of Monsanto' (29 May 2018) <https://www.justice.gov/opa/pr/justice-department-secures-largest-merger-divestiture-ever-preserve-competition-threatened> accessed 31 July 2020

M Sherman, 'How Bayer-Monsanto became one of the worst corporate deals—in 12 charts' *The Wall Street Journal* (28 August 2019) <https://ezproxy-prd.bodleian.ox.ac.uk:2186/docview/2281135814/14F24F8D5F4B4E27PQ/1?accountid=13042> (accessed 31 July 2020)

C Winter and T Loh, 'With each Roundup verdict, Bayer's Monsanto purchase looks worse' *Bloomberg* (19 September 2019) <https://www.bloomberg.com/news/features/2019-09-19/bayer-s-monsanto-purchase-looks-worse-with-each-roundup-verdict> accessed 31 July 2020

Chapter 11: The international dimension

Lotus Case (France v Turkey), P.C.I.J., Series A, No. 10 (1927)

US v Aluminum Company of America (Aloca), 148 F.2d 416 (2 Cir. 1945)

Timberlane Lumber Co. v Bank of America, 549 F.2d 596 (9 Cir. 1976)

Metro Industries Inc. v Sammi Corp, 82 F.3d 839 (9 Cir. 1996)

Hartford Fire Insurance Co. v California, 113 S. Ct. 2891 (1993)

Ahlström Osakeyhtiö and others v Commission (Wood Pulp Cartel)
(Joined Cases 89, 104, 114, 116, 117 and 125 to 129/85), [1988]
ECR 5193, [1988] 4 CMLR 407

Gencor Ltd v Commission (T-102/96), [1999] ECR II-753, [1999] 4
CMLR 971

Intel Corp. v Commission (T-286/09), [2014] 5 CMLR 9

Agreement between the European Communities and the Government
of the United States of America regarding the application of their
competition laws (23 September 1991), reprinted in 4 Trade Reg.
Rpt. (CCH) 13, 504, and OJ L95 (27 April 1995) corrected at OJ
L131/38 (15 June 1995)

US-EU Merger Working Group, 'Best practices on cooperation in
merger investigations' (2011) <https://ec.europa.eu/competition/
mergers/legislation/best_practices_2011_en.pdf> accessed
31 July 2020

The Munich Draft International Antitrust Code; reprinted in [1993]
65 Antitrust & Trade Regulation Report No. 1628

MJ Trebilcock and R Howse, *The Regulation of International Trade*
(Routledge, 2nd ed. 1998) 472

Final reflections

A Ezrachi, 'Sponge' *J of Antitrust Enforcement* 5 (2017): 49

A Ezrachi and ME Stucke, 'The fight over antitrust's soul' *J of Eur
Competition L & Policy* 9 (2017): 1

A Ezrachi and ME Stucke, 'Artificial intelligence & collusion: when
computers inhibit competition' *U of Illinois LRev* (2017): 1775

S Holmes, 'Climate change, sustainability and competition law' *J of
Antitrust Enforcement* 8 (2020): 354

Index

Note: Figures are indicated by an italic '*f*' following the Page number.

For the benefit of digital users, indexed terms that span two pages (e.g., 52–53) may, on occasion, appear on only one of those pages.

H

I

W

LAW
A Very Short Introduction
Raymond Wacks

Law underlies our society - it protects our rights, imposes duties on each of us, and establishes a framework for the conduct of almost every social, political, and economic activity. The punishment of crime, compensation of the injured, and the enforcement of contracts are merely some of the tasks of a modern legal system. It also strives to achieve justice, promote freedom, and protect our security. This *Very Short Introduction* provides a clear, jargon-free account of modern legal systems, explaining how the law works both in the Western tradition and around the world.

THE EUROPEAN UNION
A Very Short Introduction

John Pinder & Simon Usherwood

This *Very Short Introduction* explains the European Union in plain English. Fully updated for 2007 to include controversial and current topics such as the Euro currency, the EU's enlargement, and its role in ongoing world affairs, this accessible guide shows how and why the EU has developed from 1950 to the present. Covering a range of topics from the Union's early history and the ongoing interplay between 'eurosceptics' and federalists, to the single market, agriculture, and the environment, the authors examine the successes and failures of the EU, and explain the choices that lie ahead in the 21st century.

www.oup.com/vsi